# Relationship Workbook

Written by

Hector Suco

Edited by

Lucia Suco

Rachel Hillary Rosenberg

RELATIONSHIP WORKBOOK
Copyright © 2019
Written by Hector Suco
Edited by Lucia Suco and Rachel Hillary Rosenberg
All Rights Reserved.
Printed in the United States of America

This book in its entirety may not be reproduced or transmitted in any form or by any means, electronic or mechanical, including photocopying, recording or by any information storage and retrieval system, without written permission from the author.

While the author strives to make the information in this book as accurate as possible, the author makes no claims, promises, or guarantees about the accuracy, completeness, or adequacy of the contents of this book, and expressly disclaims liability for errors and omissions in the contents of this book.

The material in this book includes information by third parties. Third Party materials comprise of the opinions expressed by their owners. As such, the author of this book does not assume responsibility or liability for any Third Party Material or opinions.

Whether because of the general evolution of the Internet, or the unforeseen changes in company policy and editorial submission guidelines, what is stated as fact at the time of this writing, may become outdated or simply inapplicable at a later date. Great effort has been exerted to safeguard the accuracy of this writing.

This book is not intended as a substitute for the medical advice of physicians, including but not limited to doctors, psychiatrists, and psychologists. The reader should regularly consult a physician in matters relating to his or her health and particularly with respect to any symptoms that may require diagnosis or medical attention.

http://www.HectorSucoSpeaker.com

ISBN: 978-1-7321294-1-2

# Also by Hector Suco

The Ultimate Happiness and Gratitude Journal
Paperback

Life Worksheets
*Paperback*

Quotes For The Classroom
*Paperback*

Online Courses
(Goals, Stress, Happiness, Relationships, and more)

Life Lessons
*Motivational Spoken Word Album*

Quotes For Life
*EBook*

This book is dedicated to my wife,
Lucia Suco

# Forward

In the beginning, there were questions about relationships in general. I gave my honest opinion and that was that. Then, I began skimming through a few worksheets. Hector didn't seem to think I was done, and I somehow ended up editing this entire project! I was definitely not prepared to deal with so much information and I was quite overwhelmed at how much substance there was to this workbook.

This book has been a labor of love. Information needed gathering, options for topics needed to be hashed out, and then there was the editing and re-editing of the content. Making sure this book was as inclusive and thorough as possible was a great undertaking, as relationships.

As I read through the workbook, I noticed that, in my opinion, Hector was missing something. After having been in a non-traditional relationship myself, I didn't feel like the workbook would be complete unless it was more inclusive of non-heteronormative, non-traditional relationships. It was then that I suggested adding an Open Relationship Worksheet. I am glad Hector was open to adding it, as well as including applicable options for non-traditional relationships throughout the book.

I'm happy you're here and seeking advice. That means you've already won half the battle. You're trying to help yourself and/or your relationship. I think you, and anyone else reading, will find useful and practical information within these pages. While some of you may feel *odd* about reading this, I have two sayings I live by: "you miss 100% of the shots you don't take," and "I'll try anything once, and twice if I like it". I encourage you to use these pages to facilitate open-mindedness and communication, as these are key factors in your relationship with others as well as with yourself.

Good luck! I hope you find what you're looking for.

All the best,
Rachel Hillary Rosenberg
Editor

# Contents

| | | |
|---|---|---|
| Introduction & Preface | 1 |
| 1. Being Single | 4 |
| 2. Romantic Attraction | 12 |
| 3. Fear of Romantic Rejection | 20 |
| 4. Romantic Rejection | 25 |
| 5. Friend Zone | 31 |
| 6. Expectations | 37 |
| 7. Past Dating Experiences | 45 |
| 8. Past Relationship Experiences | 48 |
| 9. Relationship Deal Breakers | 51 |
| 10. Friends With Benefits | 59 |
| 11. Dating | 66 |
| 12. In A Relationship | 80 |
| 13. Open Relationship | 106 |
| 14. Love | 116 |
| 15. Romance | 133 |
| 16. A Relationship Letter of Gratitude | 137 |
| 17. Jealousy | 147 |
| 18. Relationship Trust | 151 |
| 19. Break Up | 157 |
| 20. Is Marriage For You | 170 |
| 21. Engagement | 178 |
| 22. Marriage | 186 |
| 23. Sex | 205 |
| 24. Relationship Finances | 213 |
| 25. Relationship Checkup | 225 |
| 26. Honesty Hour | 237 |
| 27. Relationship Conflict Resolution | 247 |
| 28. Romantic Attraction – When It Is Not Okay | 261 |
| 29. Romantic Betrayed | 269 |
| 30. Romantic Betrayer | 277 |
| 31. Marriage Separation | 287 |
| 32. Divorce | 298 |
| 33. Remarrying After Divorce | 310 |
| 34. Loss Of Partner | 316 |
| 35. Finding Partnership After Loss | 322 |

# Introduction

My life's purpose is to help people live better lives. After hearing a lot of people complain about either their own partner or the fact that they didn't have one, caused me to start one or two relationship worksheets. What started as a little side project turned into an array of relationship issues from single all the way down to finding partnership after loss.

Relationships are one of the most rewarding parts of life, but they are also one of the most difficult areas of our lives to navigate. Whether we are looking for a soul mate, recovering from a painful breakup, or trying to keep the sparks flying in our marriage, it can leave us feeling stressed, confused, and defeated, even when other aspects of our lives seem to be running smoothly.

If you have ever felt unfulfilled when it comes to love, if you have ever feel like you are stuck on a Ferris wheel of relationship's highs and lows, I want you to know that you are not alone. Like many of you, I have had my fair share of challenges when it comes to relationships. With every struggle comes the opportunity to learn, grow, and become an even better person than you were yesterday.

It is easy to let heartbreak and uncertainty paralyze us in our relationships. It is easy to become frustrated looking for answers that seem to never come. What we often do not realize is that these answers we are so desperately searching for lie within ourselves. We just need some guidance in figuring out how to identify them. That is why I created this workbook.

Through thirty-five worksheets, all aspects of relationships are covered in order to help you figure out what's blocking you. From being single, dating, and a fear of rejection to love, jealousy, and break-up worksheets are included. More serious worksheets include marriage, cheating, divorce, and moving on from the loss of a partner. Extra care was taken to make sure that this book was inclusive of non-heteronormative, non-traditional relationships.

If you are ready to self-reflect and work toward becoming the best romantic partner I know you can be, then let us get started.

# Preface

As you begin to fill out these worksheets, you can look back and see what you wrote months or years later. Not all of these worksheets will apply to you. Pick and choose which worksheets to focus on. You choose how and when to start the process. The suggested worksheets below are particularly for that issue independently. However, they are not set in stone. Someone who is divorced can also technically be single, dating, or even in a relationship. The worksheets you decide to fill out are up to you. After the worksheets, there is a guide that can clarify any questions, give examples, and/or give advice. Leave the last worksheets empty so that you can make copies if you wish to do so.

## Single

If you are single, you will be filling out these worksheets by yourself. It will be the first step in giving you a perspective of where you are now and where you want to be.

Suggested worksheets include 1 – 11.

## Dating

If you are in the dating scene, start some of the worksheets on your own. Decide if you want to share these worksheets with your prospective partner(s), maybe not on a first date, though.

Suggested worksheets include 2 – 11.

## In A Relationship

Fill these worksheets out with your partner.

Suggested worksheets include 6, 9, 12, 14 - 16, 18, 20, and 24 – 27.

# Open Relationship or Marriage

Fill these worksheets out with your partner(s).

Suggested worksheets include 9, 12 - 16, 18, and 23 – 27.

# Engaged

Fill these worksheets out with your partner.

Suggested worksheets include 14 - 16, 18, 21, and 23 – 27.

# Married

Fill these worksheets out with your partner.

Suggested worksheets include 14 - 16, 18, and 22 - 27.

# Divorced

Suggested worksheets include 31, 32, and 33.

# Widowed

Suggested worksheets include 34 and 35.

# Relationship Struggles

Worksheets include 3, 4, 17, 19, and 27 – 32.

Name:_____     Hector Suco     Date:_____

# Being Single

1. Age: _____

2. How happy are you being single?

☐ Joyful  ☐ Happy  ☐ Okay  ☐ Unhappy  ☐ Miserable

3. Do you want to be in a relationship?  ☐ Yes  ☐ No

*Yes: Answer Questions 3A, 7, 8, 9, 10, & 11*

*No: Answer Questions 3A, 4, 5, & 6*

3A. Why do/don't you want to be in a relationship?

_____

_____

4. For how long do you want to stay single?

_____

5. How would you feel if you started to develop romantic feelings for someone?

_____

6. What would you do?

_____

7. How do you search for potential dates/partners?

☐ Friends  ☐ Online  ☐ Outings  ☐ Blind Dates  ☐ Speed Dating

| 8. Do you believe in love at first sight? | ☐ Yes | ☐ No |
|---|---|---|
| 9. Have you gone on dates? | ☐ Yes (Go to #9A) | ☐ No (Go to #10) |
| 9A. Have you been dating someone consistently? | ☐ Yes (Go to #9B) | ☐ No (Go to #10) |
| 9B. Do you want to take the relationship to the next level? | ☐ Yes (Go to #9C & 9D) | ☐ No (Go to #10) |
| 9C. Have you told them? | ☐ Yes | ☐ No |
| 9D. Why or why not? _____ | | |
| 10. Do you have your eye on someone? | ☐ Yes (Go to #10A) | ☐ No |
| 10A. Have you asked them on a date? | ☐ Yes (Go to #10B) | ☐ No (Go to #10C) |
| 10B. What did they say? _____ | | |
| 10C. Why not? _____ | | |

11. What are your next steps?

_____

_____

_____

Name:_____     Hector Suco     Date:_____

# Being Single

1. Age: _____

2. How happy are you being single?

☐ Joyful     ☐ Happy     ☐ Okay     ☐ Unhappy     ☐ Miserable

3. Do you want to be in a relationship?     ☐ Yes     ☐ No

*Yes: Answer Questions 3A, 7, 8, 9, 10, & 11*

*No: Answer Questions 3A, 4, 5, & 6*

3A. Why do/don't you want to be in a relationship?

_____

_____

4. For how long do you want to stay single?

_____

5. How would you feel if you started to develop romantic feelings for someone?

_____

6. What would you do?

_____

7. How do you search for potential dates/partners?

☐ Friends     ☐ Online     ☐ Outings     ☐ Blind Dates     ☐ Speed Dating

| 8. Do you believe in love at first sight? | ☐ Yes | ☐ No |
|---|---|---|
| 9. Have you gone on dates? | ☐ Yes (Go to #9A) | ☐ No (Go to #10) |
| 9A. Have you been dating someone consistently? | ☐ Yes (Go to #9B) | ☐ No (Go to #10) |
| 9B. Do you want to take the relationship to the next level? | ☐ Yes (Go to #9C & 9D) | ☐ No (Go to #10) |
| 9C. Have you told them? | ☐ Yes | ☐ No |
| 9D. Why or why not? _____ | | |
| 10. Do you have your eye on someone? | ☐ Yes (Go to #10A) | ☐ No |
| 10A. Have you asked them on a date? | ☐ Yes (Go to #10B) | ☐ No (Go to #10C) |
| 10B. What did they say? _____ | | |
| 10C. Why not? _____ | | |

11. What are your next steps?

_____

_____

_____

Name:_____        Hector Suco        Date: _____

# Being Single

1. Age: _____

2. How happy are you being single?

☐ Joyful    ☐ Happy    ☐ Okay    ☐ Unhappy    ☐ Miserable

3. Do you want to be in a relationship?    ☐ Yes    ☐ No

*Yes: Answer Questions 3A, 7, 8, 9, 10, & 11*

*No: Answer Questions 3A, 4, 5, & 6*

3A. Why do/don't you want to be in a relationship?

_____

_____

4. For how long do you want to stay single?

_____

5. How would you feel if you started to develop romantic feelings for someone?

_____

6. What would you do?

_____

7. How do you search for potential dates/partners?

☐ Friends    ☐ Online    ☐ Outings    ☐ Blind Dates    ☐ Speed Dating

| 8. Do you believe in love at first sight? | ☐ Yes | ☐ No |
|---|---|---|
| 9. Have you gone on dates? | ☐ Yes (Go to #9A) | ☐ No (Go to #10) |
| 9A. Have you been dating someone consistently? | ☐ Yes (Go to #9B) | ☐ No (Go to #10) |
| 9B. Do you want to take the relationship to the next level? | ☐ Yes (Go to #9C & 9D) | ☐ No (Go to #10) |
| 9C. Have you told them? | ☐ Yes | ☐ No |
| 9D. Why or why not? _____ | | |
| 10. Do you have your eye on someone? | ☐ Yes (Go to #10A) | ☐ No |
| 10A. Have you asked them on a date? | ☐ Yes (Go to #10B) | ☐ No (Go to #10C) |
| 10B. What did they say? _____ | | |
| 10C. Why not? _____ | | |

11. What are your next steps?

_____

_____

_____

# Being Single Worksheet Guide

1. Being single at any age is normal. Age is just a number.

2. How happy are you in life? Does being single have an effect on your overall happiness? If it does, then you are basing your happiness on someone else. Without this "special person" in your life, are you unhappy? Happiness starts from within.

3A. Determining if you want to be in a relationship is easy. The challenging part is to figure out why.

Yes: Why do you want to be in a relationship? Examples include:

| Companionship | Sex | Fitting In | Desire to love someone | Desire to be loved |
|---|---|---|---|---|

No: Why do you want to stay single? Examples include:

| Independence | No commitment | Sexual Independence | Productivity | Personal Freedom |
|---|---|---|---|---|

4. There are some people who never want to be in a relationship. There are others that want a relationship further in life. Whichever you choose, I would suggest you to pick one that will keep you happy.

5. & 6. It can happen at any moment. One person crosses your path that you cannot keep your eye off. One person that defies everything you ever thought of. One person that breaks you (in a good way). What would you do?

7. Online: According to Nasdaq.com, in 2015, Americans spent an estimated $2 billion on online dating sites. People go out of their way to try to find that special someone, but you do not have to break the bank to do so. Make sure the money you spend is within your budget.

Outings: Asking someone for their number during an outing.

8. Love is a mix of feelings and states of mind that are associated with affection and pleasure. Since love is something considered so deep that not everyone is able to find it, most people would logically pick no. Do not mix up *love at first sight* with infatuation.

9. Regardless of whether someone has gone on dates once with multiple people, or multiple times with the same person, dating takes practice. The best way of being a good person to date is to go on many dates. However, going on dates is different than being in a committed relationship.

10. Mustering up the courage to approach someone that you have your eye on is not easy. The fear of rejection holds back a lot of people who happen to be shy. Other people feel that the person they have their eye on is a friend and by asking them out on a date, it may be the end of the friendship. When you feel that your want for a relationship will outweigh the consequences of rejection, you may want to take that next step.

11. What is next for you? Write down what you want and how you will go about doing it.

I hope this has helped you.
Good luck on your journey.

Name: _____  Hector Suco  Date: _____

# Romantic Attraction

1. What is your relationship status? _____

2. Who do you have feelings for? _____

3. How long have you had feelings for this person? _____

4. What do you like about this person?

   _____

5. How does this person feel about you?

   _____

6. What is this person's relationship status?

|   | **Status** | **Definition** | **Go To:** |
|---|---|---|---|
| ☐ | Single | Not dating or talking to anyone | #7 |
| ☐ | Dating Scene | Dating multiple people mostly once, maybe twice | #8 |
| ☐ | In A Relationship | Relationship, Engaged, or Married | #9 |

7. Have you ask them out on a date?

☐  Yes: What did they say? _____

☐  No: Why not? _____

8. Are they currently dating someone consistently?
- ☐ Yes (Go to #9)
- ☐ No (Go back to #7, then stop)

9. Is your crush happy with their current relationship? Are you sure they will want to be with you if and when they end their current relationship?

_____

_____

10. Are you willing to be the person that your crush cheats with?

_____

_____

11. How long are you willing to wait for this person?

_____

_____

12. As you wait for this person, what would you do if someone else catches your eye?

_____

_____

Name: _____   Hector Suco   Date: _____

# Romantic Attraction

1. What is your relationship status? _____

2. Who do you have feelings for? _____

3. How long have you had feelings for this person? _____

4. What do you like about this person?

_____

5. How does this person feel about you?

_____

6. What is this person's relationship status?

|   | **Status** | **Definition** | **Go To:** |
|---|---|---|---|
| ☐ | Single | Not dating or talking to anyone | #7 |
| ☐ | Dating Scene | Dating multiple people mostly once, maybe twice | #8 |
| ☐ | In A Relationship | Relationship, Engaged, or Married | #9 |

7. Have you ask them out on a date?

☐   Yes: What did they say? _____

☐   No: Why not? _____

14

8. Are they currently dating someone consistently?
- ☐ Yes (Go to #9)
- ☐ No (Go back to #7, then stop)

9. Is your crush happy with their current relationship? Are you sure they will want to be with you if and when they end their current relationship?

_____

_____

10. Are you willing to be the person that your crush cheats with?

_____

_____

11. How long are you willing to wait for this person?

_____

_____

12. As you wait for this person, what would you do if someone else catches your eye?

_____

_____

Name: _____    Hector Suco    Date: _____

# Romantic Attraction

1. What is your relationship status? _____

2. Who do you have feelings for? _____

3. How long have you had feelings for this person? _____

4. What do you like about this person?

_____

5. How does this person feel about you?

_____

6. What is this person's relationship status?

|   | **Status** | **Definition** | **Go To:** |
|---|---|---|---|
| ☐ | Single | Not dating or talking to anyone | #7 |
| ☐ | Dating Scene | Dating multiple people mostly once, maybe twice | #8 |
| ☐ | In A Relationship | Relationship, Engaged, or Married | #9 |

7. Have you ask them out on a date?

☐ Yes: What did they say? _____

☐ No: Why not? _____

16

8. Are they currently dating someone consistently?
- ☐ Yes (Go to #9)
- ☐ No (Go back to #7)

9. Is your crush happy with their current relationship? Are you sure they will want to be with you if and when they end their current relationship?

_____

_____

10. Are you willing to be the person that your crush cheats with?

_____

_____

11. How long are you willing to wait for this person?

_____

_____

12. As you wait for this person, what would you do if someone else catches your eye?

_____

_____

# Romantic Attraction Worksheet Guide

2. Write down the person's name.

3. The length of time you have had feelings for this person matters. Feelings strengthen with time, but try not to find yourself looking at their social media profiles on a daily basis. Just get to know them.

4. What are the qualities that attract you about this person? Examples include:

| Looks/Body | Confidence | Personality | Caring | Adventurous |
|---|---|---|---|---|
| Financial Stability | Family-Oriented | Social Status | Good Chemistry | Outgoing |

5. This is a tough question because you are not that person. This question could be answered if you ask them or if you ask one of their friends, "How do they feel about me?" If you do not know, leave this blank or give your best guess. If you know they do not feel the same way about you, you might want to let them go or try to stay friends. Be careful with staying in a state of infatuation. It is unhealthy to obsess over the thought of being with someone.

6. Your crush's relationship status is important. They may be happy right where they are in life.

7. If they are single, then the questions that follow are simple. Writing down your answers can be therapeutic. Have you asked them out on a date or told them how you feel? If yes, how did they respond? If not, why not? What are you waiting for? Be careful with staying in a state of infatuation. It is unhealthy to obsess over the thought of being with someone.

8. If your crush is not dating someone consistently, you have a green light to ask them out. If your crush is dating someone consistently, then you must tread lightly. You must assume that they are in a relationship already even if it is not "official" yet. You can politely ask them if their relationship is serious. It will give you a good idea as to how much time you must muster up the courage to ask them out or tell them how you feel. Do not wait or it may be too late.

9. You will not be able to answer this question unless you ask them directly. This might be a little off-putting because at the end of the day, it is none of your business. Try to be honest with yourself as this question leads into the other questions.

10. How would you feel being "that person"? Are you willing to put your reputation on the line for your crush? Would you want someone to do that to you?

11. Are you willing to wait for your crush to be ready to date or to end their relationship? For how long?

12. Are you willing to move on if someone else catches your eye? If not, you might be selling yourself short. You owe it to yourself to try new things and go on dates. If your crush is truly happy, wouldn't you want them to stay that way and maybe find someone like they have?

I hope this has helped you.
Good luck on your journey.

Name: _____    Hector Suco    Date: _____

# Fear of Romantic Rejection

1. Have you been rejected before?   ☐ Yes   ☐ No
Yes: How did it make you feel?

_____

2. Is the person you want to ask out a friend of yours?   ☐ Yes   ☐ No
Yes: Do you fear that if you ask them out and they reject   ☐ Yes   ☐ No
you, your friendship with them will change or end?
Yes: Who do you think will end the friendship, you or your friend? Why?

_____

3. Do you like to stay in your comfort zone or take risks? _____
Write down what you are thinking as you contemplate whether to tell them how you feel or ask them out.

_____

_____

4. Write down how you feel if they would reject you.

_____

_____

5. What would you say to a friend who was rejected?

_____

_____

6. Do you think rejection is a part of life?   ☐ Yes   ☐ No

7. Do you think rejection can make someone stronger?   ☐ Yes   ☐ No

Name: _____  Hector Suco  Date: _____

# Fear of Romantic Rejection

1. Have you been rejected before?  ☐ Yes  ☐ No
Yes: How did it make you feel?
_____

2. Is the person you want to ask out a friend of yours?  ☐ Yes  ☐ No
Yes: Do you fear that if you ask them out and they reject  ☐ Yes  ☐ No
you, your friendship with them will change or end?
Yes: Who do you think will end the friendship, you or your friend? Why?
_____

3. Do you like to stay in your comfort zone or take risks? _____
Write down what you are thinking as you contemplate whether or not to tell them how you feel or ask them out.

_____

_____

4. Write down how you feel if they would reject you.

_____

_____

5. What would you say to a friend who was rejected?

_____

_____

6. Do you think rejection is a part of life?  ☐ Yes  ☐ No
7. Do you think rejection can make someone stronger?  ☐ Yes  ☐ No

Name: _____     Hector Suco     Date: _____

# Fear of Romantic Rejection

1. Have you been rejected before?  ☐ Yes    ☐ No

Yes: How did it make you feel?

_____

2. Is the person you want to ask out a friend of yours?   ☐ Yes   ☐ No
Yes: Do you fear that if you ask them out and they reject   ☐ Yes   ☐ No
you, your friendship with them will change or end?
Yes: Who do you think will end the friendship, you or your friend? Why?

_____

3. Do you like to stay in your comfort zone or take risks? _____
Write down what you are thinking as you contemplate whether or not to tell them how you feel or ask them out.

_____

_____

4. Write down how you feel if they would reject you.

_____

_____

5. What would you say to a friend who was rejected?

_____

_____

6. Do you think rejection is a part of life?   ☐ Yes   ☐ No

7. Do you think rejection can make someone stronger?   ☐ Yes   ☐ No

Name: _____    Hector Suco    Date: _____

# Fear of Romantic Rejection

1. Have you been rejected before?  ☐ Yes  ☐ No
Yes: How did it make you feel?

_____

2. Is the person you want to ask out a friend of yours?   ☐ Yes  ☐ No
Yes: Do you fear that if you ask them out and they reject   ☐ Yes  ☐ No
you, your friendship with them will change or end?
Yes: Who do you think will end the friendship, you or your friend? Why?

_____

3. Do you like to stay in your comfort zone or take risks? _____
Write down what you are thinking as you contemplate whether or not to tell them how you feel or ask them out.

_____

_____

4. Write down how you feel if they would reject you.

_____

_____

5. What would you say to a friend who was rejected?

_____

_____

6. Do you think rejection is a part of life?   ☐ Yes  ☐ No

7. Do you think rejection can make someone stronger?   ☐ Yes  ☐ No

# Fear of Romantic Rejection Worksheet Guide

1. Analyzing how you feel can help you understand yourself and can possibly alter your viewpoint. Self-reflecting is a very healthy practice and can help you change for the better.

3. The fear of rejection is, in essence, a fear. It is a response to perceived danger. We can face our fears or run from them, but we are ultimately the ones that create them and destroy them.

"Fear is not real. The only place fear can exist is in our thoughts of the future. It is a product of our imagination, causing us to fear things that do not at present and may not exist. That is near insanity. Do not misunderstand me, danger is very real, but fear is a choice."
-Will Smith as Cypher Raige from the film "After Earth"

"Life begins at the end of your comfort zone."
-Neale Donald Walsch

4. If they reject you, how would you feel? There is no solution here, just an exercise to pull these thoughts out of your head and give you a chance to see them written out on paper.

5. This is a good practice and it could definitely be used as advice to yourself as well as your friend. "There are other fish in the sea," works very well here.

6. & 7. In my opinion, rejection is a part of life. Jia Jiang of fearbuster.com came up with his 100 Days of Rejection Therapy in which he goes out to purposely get rejected. "My goal is to desensitize myself from the pain of rejection and overcome my fear." Everything from asking $100 from a stranger to requesting a "burger refill" are part of the process. The more it happened, the less it hurt.

I hope this has helped you.
Good luck on your journey.

Name: _____  Hector Suco   Date: _____

# Romantic Rejection

1. Age: _____

2. Who rejected you? _____

3. What reasons did they give you for their decision?

_____

_____

4. What do you think is the real reason they rejected you?

_____

_____

_____

5. Do you think you are now in the Friend Zone?   ☐ Yes (Go to #5A)   ☐ No

5A. Why do you think this?

_____

| | | |
|---|---|---|
| 6. Would you try to ask them out again? | ☐ Yes | ☐ No |
| 7. Do you think rejection is a part of life? | ☐ Yes | ☐ No |
| 8. Do you think rejections can make someone stronger? | ☐ Yes | ☐ No |
| 9. Do you think there are "other fish in the sea"? | ☐ Yes | ☐ No |
| 10. Do you fear being rejected again? | ☐ Yes | ☐ No |

Name: _____    Hector Suco    Date: _____

# Romantic Rejection

1. Age: _____

2. Who rejected you? _____

3. What reasons did they give you for their decision?

_____

_____

4. What do you think is the real reason they rejected you?

_____

_____

_____

5. Do you think you are now in the Friend Zone?    ☐ Yes (Go to #5A)    ☐ No

5A. Why do you think this?

_____

| | | |
|---|---|---|
| 6. Would you try to ask them out again? | ☐ Yes | ☐ No |
| 7. Do you think rejection is a part of life? | ☐ Yes | ☐ No |
| 8. Do you think rejections can make someone stronger? | ☐ Yes | ☐ No |
| 9. Do you think there are "other fish in the sea"? | ☐ Yes | ☐ No |
| 10. Do you fear being rejected again? | ☐ Yes | ☐ No |

Name: _____    Hector Suco    Date: _____

# Romantic Rejection

1. Age: _____

2. Who rejected you? _____

3. What reasons did they give you for their decision?
_____
_____

4. What do you think is the real reason they rejected you?
_____
_____
_____

5. Do you think you are now in the Friend Zone?    ☐ Yes (Go to #5A)    ☐ No

5A. Why do you think this?
_____

| | | |
|---|---|---|
| 6. Would you try to ask them out again? | ☐ Yes | ☐ No |
| 7. Do you think rejection is a part of life? | ☐ Yes | ☐ No |
| 8. Do you think rejections can make someone stronger? | ☐ Yes | ☐ No |
| 9. Do you think there are "other fish in the sea"? | ☐ Yes | ☐ No |
| 10. Do you fear being rejected again? | ☐ Yes | ☐ No |

Name: _____   Hector Suco   Date: _____

# Romantic Rejection

1. Age: _____

2. Who rejected you? _____

3. What reasons did they give you for their decision?
   _____
   _____

4. What do you think is the real reason they rejected you?
   _____
   _____
   _____

5. Do you think you are now in the Friend Zone?   ☐ Yes (Go to #5A)   ☐ No

5A. Why do you think this?
   _____

6. Would you try to ask them out again?   ☐ Yes   ☐ No

7. Do you think rejection is a part of life?   ☐ Yes   ☐ No

8. Do you think rejections can make someone stronger?   ☐ Yes   ☐ No

9. Do you think there are "other fish in the sea"?   ☐ Yes   ☐ No

10. Do you fear being rejected again?   ☐ Yes   ☐ No

# Romantic Rejection Worksheet Guide

3. Examples include:

| They are not ready for a relationship | You are coming on too strong | "You are like the rest" | There's someone else | You only want the physical |
|---|---|---|---|---|
| They are turned off | They do not want to ruin friendship | You are not their type | You are too intense | There is an addiction problem |

4. Give your honest opinion about why you think they rejected you. Try not to put the blame solely on them or you. Do not pity yourself, but do not be too overconfident either.

5. Being put in the Friend Zone is a curse and a blessing. The curse is not being able to fulfill your want to be in a relationship. The blessing, depending on how you see it, is the fact that you may have another chance in the future. Decide how close you want to be with them or decide to ultimately let them go.

6. You may ask someone out once, twice, but not a third time. The third time will make you seem clingy, desperate, or worse.

I have heard stories of men who have asked their current wives out on a date dozens of times before they said yes. You have to gauge the situation and your crush's response. If it is a soft no, then you may want to try again another time. A hard, "No and do not ever ask me again," could lead to a restraining order.

7. & 8. Rejection is a part of life and it does make us stronger. Jia Jiang of fearbuster.com came up with his 100 Days of Rejection Therapy in which he goes out to purposely get rejected. "My goal is to desensitize myself from the pain of rejection and overcome my fear." He does everything from asking $100 from a stranger to requesting a "burger refill."

9. My wife asked me one day, "do you think there is someone for everyone?" I replied, "if someone's chances of finding a date is 'one in a million,' and there are more than seven billion people in the world, then there are more than 7,000 people that would date them." All kidding aside, there are plenty of fish in the sea. Believe it and go fishing.

10. Usually, people who fear any type of rejection like to stay in their comfort zone. Fear of rejection is natural, but do not let it control you. Use my Fear of Romantic Rejection Worksheet to further explore your feelings.

I hope this has helped you.
Good luck on your journey.

Name: _____  Hector Suco   Date: _____

# Friend Zone

1. What is your friend's name? _____

2. What do you want in the long run?

   ☐ A Relationship      ☐ To Be Friends With Benefits      ☐ A One Night Stand

3. Is your friend currently in a relationship?
   ☐ Yes
   ☐ Yes, but they are about to break up
   ☐ No, but they are talking to/dating someone else
   ☐ No

4. Have you told your friend how you feel?

   ☐ Yes
   ☐ No: Why not? _____
      Are you planning to tell them? When? _____

5. Have they told you "let's just be friends"?

   ☐ Yes: How did you respond? _____
   ☐ No: What did they say or do to make you think that you are in the friend zone?
   _____

6. Do you believe there is a chance they may see you as more than a friend?

   ☐ Yes: How long are you willing to wait? _____

   ☐ No: Why? _____

| | | |
|---|---|---|
| 7. Would you go on other dates in the meantime? | ☐ Yes | ☐ No |
| 7A. Has your friend encouraged you to go on other dates? | ☐ Yes | ☐ No |
| 7B. Has your friend told you, "please do not wait for me"? | ☐ Yes | ☐ No |
| 8. Would you pursue someone new if they catch your eye? | ☐ Yes | ☐ No |
| 8A. Would you give your friend an ultimatum? | ☐ Yes | ☐ No |

Name: _____    Hector Suco    Date: _____

# Friend Zone

1. What is your friend's name? _____

2. What do you want in the long run?

   ☐ A Relationship      ☐ To Be Friends With Benefits      ☐ A One Night Stand

3. Is your friend currently in a relationship?
   ☐ Yes
   ☐ Yes, but they are about to break up
   ☐ No, but they are talking to/dating someone else
   ☐ No

4. Have you told your friend how you feel?

   ☐ Yes
   ☐ No: Why not? _____
       Are you planning to tell them? When? _____

5. Have they told you "let's just be friends"?

   ☐ Yes: How did you respond? _____
   ☐ No: What did they say or do to make you think that you are in the friend zone?
   _____

6. Do you believe there is a chance they may see you as more than a friend?

   ☐ Yes: How long are you willing to wait? _____

   ☐ No: Why? _____

| | | |
|---|---|---|
| 7. Would you go on other dates in the meantime? | ☐ Yes | ☐ No |
| 7A. Has your friend encouraged you to go on other dates? | ☐ Yes | ☐ No |
| 7B. Has your friend told you, "please do not wait for me"? | ☐ Yes | ☐ No |
| 8. Would you pursue someone new if they catch your eye? | ☐ Yes | ☐ No |
| 8A. Would you give your friend an ultimatum? | ☐ Yes | ☐ No |

Name: _____     Hector Suco     Date: _____

# Friend Zone

1. What is your friend's name? _____

2. What do you want in the long run?

   ☐ A Relationship      ☐ To Be Friends With Benefits      ☐ A One Night Stand

3. Is your friend currently in a relationship?
   ☐ Yes
   ☐ Yes, but they are about to break up
   ☐ No, but they are talking to/dating someone else
   ☐ No

4. Have you told your friend how you feel?

   ☐ Yes
   ☐ No: Why not? _____
       Are you planning to tell them? When? _____

5. Have they told you "let's just be friends"?

   ☐ Yes: How did you respond? _____
   ☐ No: What did they say or do to make you think that you are in the friend zone?
   _____

6. Do you believe there is a chance they may see you as more than a friend?

   ☐ Yes: How long are you willing to wait? _____

   ☐ No: Why? _____

| | | |
|---|---|---|
| 7. Would you go on other dates in the meantime? | ☐ Yes | ☐ No |
| 7A. Has your friend encouraged you to go on other dates? | ☐ Yes | ☐ No |
| 7B. Has your friend told you, "please do not wait for me"? | ☐ Yes | ☐ No |
| 8. Would you pursue someone new if they catch your eye? | ☐ Yes | ☐ No |
| 8A. Would you give your friend an ultimatum? | ☐ Yes | ☐ No |

# Friend Zone Worksheet Guide

2. Relationship: You want a committed relationship.

Friends With Benefits: Friends with benefits are two friends who have a sexual relationship, but are not exclusive. If this is what is important for you, know about the risks physically and emotionally. Physically, you need to use protection to prevent STD's, STI's, and unwanted pregnancies. Emotionally, you need to be able to stay unattached while still sharing intimacy.

A One-Night Stand: If you are someone's friend just to see if you can get into their pants, you are clearly not looking for commitment. I understand that the chase is important, but it brings out a caveman/survivalist urge to hunt your prey and conquer it. That leads to treating others like pieces of meat. Is that what you want in life? Will this make you happy? What's in it for you in the long run? If this is what's important for you, know about the risks physically and emotionally. You need to use protection to prevent STD's, STI's, and unwanted pregnancies. You also need to be able to put your feelings aside despite the intimacy you will be sharing.

3. Your friend's relationship status is an important factor. If they are in a relationship or are about to break up, the length of their current relationship matters. There is a period your friend needs to go through without being in a relationship. Jumping from one relationship to another is unhealthy and they are probably going to want some space. If they are talking to someone else, you need to be honest with them about how you feel soon if you want to have a chance with them.

4. No: Mustering up the courage to approach someone that you have feelings for is not easy. Fear of rejection holds back a lot of people who happen to be shy. There are some people who feel that the person they have their eye on is a friend; they believe that by asking them out on a date and consequentially being rejected, may be the end of the friendship. Your want for a relationship with your friend may outweigh the emotional consequences of losing your friend. If this happens, you may want to take that next step. If it does not, then you will probably stay in the friend zone indefinitely.

5. Yes: How you responded to "let's just be friends" can determine the future you two have. If you told them that you cannot be their friend anymore without a relationship, you need to be sure you will be happy with that choice. If you said you were okay, then there's still a chance.

No: Did they tell you:

- I want a relationship with you, just not now
- I'm not ready (to commit)
- I do not believe in relationships
- Let's just be friends with benefits
- Other

6. I waited six months for a friend to decide if she wanted to be with me before I decided I did not want to wait anymore. I only regret it to a certain extent. Try to be happy with your situation and do not make another person responsible for your happiness. Happiness starts from within.

No: Did they tell you, "I do not like you," "I do not find you attractive," "You're not my type," or something similar? If they did, it is time to let go or keep them as a friend. There may be a chance they will see you in a different light down the road.

Do you feel that you are ugly? Has anyone told you that you look ugly? If you feel ugly, you need to work on your self-esteem. If anyone has told you that you look ugly, remember that beauty is in the eye of the beholder. Try to surround yourself with people who will support you and not bring you down.

7. "There are plenty fish in the sea," is a wise proverb. Ask your friend how they feel about you going on dates. The friend who I was waiting for told me to go out with other people. If they tell you **not** to go out on other dates, then you should ask them why they do not want you to go out with other people. If they do not want to date you then they have no right to tell you what to do. Also, try not to date others just to pass the time as you wait for your friend. It is not fair to those you are dating.

8. If someone catches your eye and your emotions are higher for them than that of your friend, the decision will be easy. The tough part is if your emotions are still as strong for your friend, even if someone else tries to come into your life. You will have to wrestle with your emotions and ultimately choose one that will make you happy. Try not to settle. In the film *Along Came Polly*, the main character falls for two different people. He knew he needed to make a decision so he wrote down the positive and negative traits of both women. This might be an exercise you can try, but this is not something you want to show to either person you are thinking about. Also, you have every right to give your friend an ultimatum with a reasonable timeline.

I hope this has helped you.
Good luck on your journey.

Name: _____   Hector Suco   Date: _____

# Expectations

This worksheet is for anyone who is expecting for their partner to take the relationship to the next level.

PYTW – Person You're Talking With

1. Age:_____

2. What is your relationship status?   ☐ Single (Go to #4)   ☐ In A Relationship

3. Do you consider yourself to be "in love" with your partner or the PYTW?

_____

4. Are you currently expecting your partner or the PYTW to take the next step in your relationship?

   ☐ Yes: What is it?   ☐ Become Official   ☐ Propose   ☐ Get Married

      ☐ Have A Child   ☐ Other: _____

☐ No:   Are you happy with your relationship status? _____ (Go to #9)

4A. Have you told your partner or the PYTW that you want to take your relationship to the next level?

_____

5. Have you given your partner or the PYTW a timetable to take the next step in the relationship?

☐ Yes:  How long did you give? _____ How long do they have left? _____

☐ No:   Are you happy with your relationship status? _____

6. Will you break off the relationship if that deadline runs out? _____

7. What is it that they want? Have they expressed the want to take the next step?

_____

8. If you are expecting for someone to take your relationship to the next level, ask them this question that Steve Harvey suggests: "I would like to ask you a hypothetical question: How would you feel if you never saw me again?"
Write about the interaction below:

_____

_____

9. Do you want children?   ☐ Yes (Go to 9A)       ☐ No

9A. How many? _____

9B. At what age do you want your first child? _____

9C. At what age do you want your last child? _____

10. Are you sexually involved with this person in an attempt to convince them to stay with you and/or take your relationship to the next level? Do you think they are aware of this? Do you think they are taking advantage of you?

_____

_____

# Speeding Up

11. Have you ever thought of speeding up the wait time by coercing your partner or the PYTW through deception or manipulation? For example, using pregnancy to keep the relationship.        ☐ Yes   ☐ No

12. There's a fine line between coercion and abuse. Are you currently on a plan to convince your partner or the PYTW to take the next step in the relationship?
        ☐ Yes (Go to #13)  ☐ No

13. What is the plan? _____

_____

14. Do you think the actions you are taking are based on a lie?
        ☐ Yes (Go to #15)  ☐ No

15. If this plan is successful, are you okay with the fact that your relationship will continue because of this lie?
        ☐ Yes           ☐ No

Name: _____  Hector Suco  Date: _____

# Expectations

This worksheet is for anyone who is expecting for their partner to take the relationship to the next level.

PYTW – Person You're Talking With

1. Age:_____

2. What is your relationship status?  ☐ Single (Go to #4)   ☐ In A Relationship

3. Do you consider yourself to be "in love" with your partner or the PYTW?

_____

4. Are you currently expecting your partner or the PYTW to take the next step in your relationship?

   ☐ Yes: What is it?   ☐ Become Official   ☐ Propose   ☐ Get Married

      ☐ Have A Child   ☐ Other: _____

☐ No:   Are you happy with your relationship status? _____ (Go to #9)

4A. Have you told your partner or the PYTW that you want to take your relationship to the next level?

_____

5. Have you given your partner or the PYTW a timetable to take the next step in the relationship?

☐ Yes:  How long did you give? _____ How long do they have left? _____

☐ No:  Are you happy with your relationship status? _____

6. Will you break off the relationship if that deadline runs out? _____

7. What is it that they want? Have they expressed the want to take the next step?

_____

8. If you are expecting for someone to take your relationship to the next level, ask them this question that Steve Harvey suggests: "I would like to ask you a hypothetical question: How would you feel if you never saw me again?"
Write about the interaction below:

_____

_____

9. Do you want children?   ☐ Yes (Go to 9A)   ☐ No

9A. How many? _____

9B. At what age do you want your first child? _____

9C. At what age do you want your last child? _____

10. Are you sexually involved with this person in an attempt to convince them to stay with you and/or take your relationship to the next level? Do you think they are aware of this? Do you think they are taking advantage of you?

_____

_____

## Speeding Up

11. Have you ever thought of speeding up the wait time by coercing your partner or the PYTW through deception or manipulation? For example, using pregnancy to keep the relationship.   ☐ Yes   ☐ No

12. There's a fine line between coercion and abuse. Are you currently on a plan to convince your partner or the PYTW to take the next step in the relationship?
   ☐ Yes (Go to #13)  ☐ No

13. What is the plan? _____

_____

14. Do you think the actions you are taking are based on a lie?
   ☐ Yes (Go to #15)  ☐ No

15. If this plan is successful, are you okay with the fact that your relationship will continue because of this lie?
   ☐ Yes         ☐ No

Name: _____  Hector Suco  Date: _____

# Expectations

This worksheet is for anyone who is expecting for their partner to take the relationship to the next level.

PYTW – Person You're Talking With

1. Age:_____

2. What is your relationship status?  ☐ Single (Go to #4)  ☐ In A Relationship

3. Do you consider yourself to be "in love" with your partner or the PYTW?

_____

4. Are you currently expecting your partner or the PYTW to take the next step in your relationship?

    ☐ Yes: What is it?  ☐ Become Official  ☐ Propose  ☐ Get Married

        ☐ Have A Child  ☐ Other: _____

☐ No:  Are you happy with your relationship status? _____ (Go to #9)

4A. Have you told your partner or the PYTW that you want to take your relationship to the next level?

_____

5. Have you given your partner or the PYTW a timetable to take the next step in the relationship?

☐ Yes:  How long did you give? _____ How long do they have left? _____

☐ No:  Are you happy with your relationship status? _____

6. Will you break off the relationship if that deadline runs out? _____

7. What is it that they want? Have they expressed the want to take the next step?

_____

8. If you are expecting for someone to take your relationship to the next level, ask them this question that Steve Harvey suggests: "I would like to ask you a hypothetical question: How would you feel if you never saw me again?"
Write about the interaction below:

_____

_____

9. Do you want children?   ☐ Yes (Go to 9A)    ☐ No

9A. How many? _____

9B. At what age do you want your first child? _____

9C. At what age do you want your last child? _____

10. Are you sexually involved with this person in an attempt to convince them to stay with you and/or take your relationship to the next level? Do you think they are aware of this? Do you think they are taking advantage of you?

_____

_____

# Speeding Up

11. Have you ever thought of speeding up the wait time by coercing your partner or the PYTW through deception or manipulation? For example, using pregnancy to keep the relationship.    ☐ Yes   ☐ No

12. There's a fine line between coercion and abuse. Are you currently on a plan to convince your partner or the PYTW to take the next step in the relationship?
☐ Yes (Go to #13) ☐ No

13. What is the plan? _____

_____

14. Do you think the actions you are taking are based on a lie?
☐ Yes (Go to #15) ☐ No

15. If this plan is successful, are you okay with the fact that your relationship will continue because of this lie?
☐ Yes        ☐ No

# Expectations Worksheet Guide

1. Age is a very important factor when determining your goals, especially when it comes to having children (if that is your end goal). This worksheet will look completely different for someone in their early 20s than for someone in their mid 30s.

2. Single: This worksheet is not necessarily for single people unless they are "talking to" or "dating" someone. In the early talking stages of a relationship, the only talk about children should be the amount each wants. The continuous talk about prospective children might turn the other person off by having them think that it is going way too fast. Remember the word "talking," not "planning."

The talk about children can go up a level when dating because specific goals can be discussed. You do not want to be wasting your time with someone who does not want children when you want two. This is a deal breaker and if the person you are dating is not comfortable with your goals, then you should end the relationship. The faster the relationship ends, the quicker you will meet someone who is more in line with your goals. If you think you can change this person's opinions about having children, it is possible, but how likely? If you want to take on this task, good luck.

In a relationship: If you are expecting your SO or the PYTW to take the next step in your relationship, this worksheet is for you.

3. A relationship is when you have two people with different pasts, paths, ideas, values, personalities and goals coming together to experience companionship, respect and love. Communication is key when developing these mutual connections, especially goals. Make sure you know what your partner's life goals are and make sure they know what yours are. Come together and see how they mash up with yours. The phrase "Love trumps all" is important here. Are you in love with your partner? Is there anything you would not do for your partner? How about waiting? Here is the fork in the road. For most women, having children is a life goal. Finding someone whom they love and having that someone love them back is also a life goal for many women. So which one is stronger? Which one takes precedent? Is the wait time causing you to fall out of love with your partner? Do you think it is a question of sacrifice? That s/he doesn't love you enough to make probably the biggest sacrifice of their lives? Ultimately, how long you wait will be based on how strong your love is for this person.

4. I am assuming that "propose" will be picked more often than not. Women have every right to ask a man when he's planning to propose. Giving them an ultimatum is also okay based on your relationship, feelings, timetable, and life goals.

5. I agree with a timetable. This would make some uncomfortable, but it does give them a choice and puts them behind the wheel. Plus, six months is more than enough time to give them.

6. Obviously, every relationship is different. The timetables will be different for each individual. Here is a range that Amy Webb came up with to guide you:

| | |
|---|---|
| Becoming Official: | 1 – 2 months |
| Propose: | 6 – 12 months |
| Getting Married: | 6 – 12 months |
| Having Kids: | 1 – 2 years |

Amy Webb heads the digital strategy house Webbmedia Group and is a founder of the SparkCamp discussion series. She's the author of "Data: A Love Story." She has a TED Talk titled "How I hacked online dating" She mentions that the whole process could be as long as 5 years. The timetables you choose will highly depend on your age.

7. This goes back to number 3 and your life's goals. Ultimately, if your goal of having children is higher than finding the love of your life, than breaking off the relationship may be the answer. If at this time, your SO or the PYTW asks for more time, gauge how serious they are by asking for a certainty: a promise ring, a contract, moving in with each other, etc.

8. This is the key to any relationship. If someone is okay with never seeing you again, there really wasn't anything there to begin with.

10. Giving the partner sex in the hopes of them staying with you is wrong. The repercussions are endless. From them taking advantage to you to you not being fulfilled and/or feeling unwanted. It is a vicious cycle of convincing yourself that it is worth it for the hope of true love. Unrequited love is a painful journey to go on. Move on and find someone that will love you with or without intimacy.

11., 12., 14., and 15. If you picked yes, I would urge you to reconsider.

13. Plans include everything from lying, threats, intimidation, possessiveness, etc. Examples include faking a pregnancy test, giving sex than stopping once married, feelings of guilt, etc.

I hope this has helped you.
Good luck with your journey.

Name: _____  Hector Suco  Date: _____

# Past Dating Experiences

This log is for you to reflect on your past dating experiences. Starting with the most recent dating experience, fill out each 5-question section and write down information that may help your experiences in the future.

1. Who did you date? _____
2. How many dates have you gone on with this person? _____
3. How would you rate their looks?

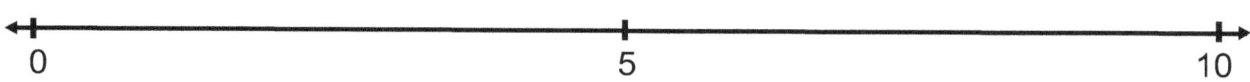

4. How would your rate their personality?

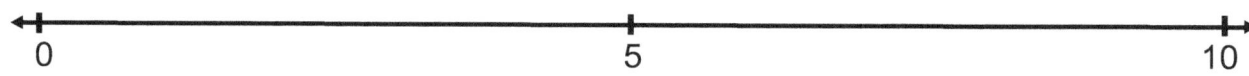

5. Why did you stop dating them?

_____

_____


1. Who did you date? _____
2. How many dates have you gone on with this person? _____
3. How would you rate their looks?

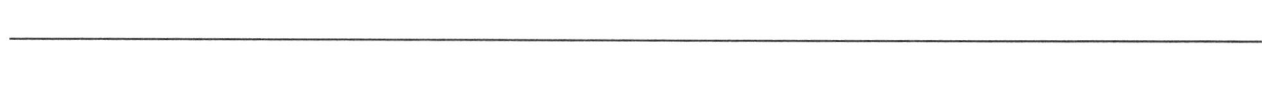

4. How would your rate their personality?

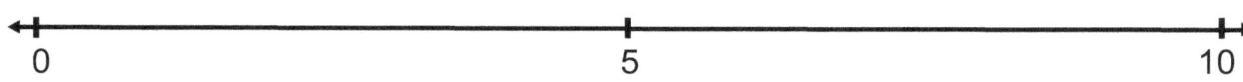

5. Why did you stop dating them?

_____

_____

1. Who did you date? _____
2. How many dates have you gone on with this person? _____
3. How would you rate their looks?

```
<+----------------------+----------------------+>
0                       5                      10
```

4. How would your rate their personality?

```
<+----------------------+----------------------+>
0                       5                      10
```

5. Why did you stop dating them?

_____

_____




1. Who did you date? _____
2. How many dates have you gone on with this person? _____
3. How would you rate their looks?

```
<+----------------------+----------------------+>
0                       5                      10
```

4. How would your rate their personality?

```
<+----------------------+----------------------+>
0                       5                      10
```

5. Why did you stop dating them?

_____

_____

1. Who did you date? _____
2. How many dates have you gone on with this person? _____
3. How would you rate their looks?

```
<--+--------------------+--------------------+-->
   0                    5                    10
```

4. How would your rate their personality?

```
<--+--------------------+--------------------+-->
   0                    5                    10
```

5. Why did you stop dating them?

_____

_____




1. Who did you date? _____
2. How many dates have you gone on with this person? _____
3. How would you rate their looks?

```
<--+--------------------+--------------------+-->
   0                    5                    10
```

4. How would your rate their personality?

```
<--+--------------------+--------------------+-->
   0                    5                    10
```

5. Why did you stop dating them?

_____

_____

Name: _____  Hector Suco  Date: _____

# Past Relationships Experiences

This log is for you to reflect on your past relationship experiences. Starting with the most recent relationship, fill out each 5-question section and write down information that may help your experiences in the future.

1. Who were you in a relationship with? _____

2. How long was this relationship? _____

3. What was the main issue in the relationship?

_____

_____

4. Who broke up with whom?
☐ I broke up with them          ☐ They broke up with me
   ☐ Mutual

5. What was/were the lesson(s) learned from this experience?

_____

_____

1. Who were you in a relationship with? _____

2. How long was this relationship? _____

3. What was the main issue in the relationship?

_____

_____

4. Who broke up with whom?

☐ I broke up with them    ☐ They broke up with me

☐ Mutual

5. What was/were the lesson(s) learned from this experience?

_____

_____

1. Who were you in a relationship with? _____

2. How long was this relationship? _____

3. What was the main issue in the relationship?

_____

_____

4. Who broke up with whom?

☐ I broke up with them    ☐ They broke up with me

☐ Mutual

5. What was/were the lesson(s) learned from this experience?

_____

_____

1. Who were you in a relationship with? _____

2. How long was this relationship? _____

3. What was the main issue in the relationship?

_____

_____

4. Who broke up with whom?

☐ I broke up with them    ☐ They broke up with me

☐ Mutual

5. What was/were the lesson(s) learned from this experience?

_____

_____

1. Who were you in a relationship with? _____

2. How long was this relationship? _____

3. What was the main issue in the relationship?

_____

_____

4. Who broke up with whom?

☐ I broke up with them    ☐ They broke up with me

☐ Mutual

5. What was/were the lesson(s) learned from this experience?

_____

_____

Name: _____    Hector Suco    Date: _____

# Relationship Deal Breakers

Deal breakers are topics (potential) couples need to hash out before moving forward in their relationship. You may want to do this worksheet with your partner to spark a conversation. If you fill this out alone, you can use it to find out what you need from your other half before you start looking for a partner.

For #1 – 12, circle 1 – 10 based on how important each are in your life with 1 being the least important and 10 being extremely important. Then, write how important they are to you when it comes to your partner.

1. Having children                     1  2  3  4  5  6  7  8  9  10

_____

_____

2. How you raise your children         1  2  3  4  5  6  7  8  9  10

_____

_____

3. Life goals                          1  2  3  4  5  6  7  8  9  10

_____

_____

4. Religion                            1  2  3  4  5  6  7  8  9  10

_____

_____

5. Where to live or settle down        1  2  3  4  5  6  7  8  9  10

_____

_____

6. Finances                                    1   2   3   4   5   6   7   8   9   10

_____

_____

7. Taste in music, movies, TV                  1   2   3   4   5   6   7   8   9   10

_____

_____

8. Politics                                    1   2   3   4   5   6   7   8   9   10

_____

_____

9. Travel. Vacations                           1   2   3   4   5   6   7   8   9   10

_____

_____

10. Sex                                        1   2   3   4   5   6   7   8   9   10

_____

_____

11. Occupation                                 1   2   3   4   5   6   7   8   9   10

_____

_____

12. Abuse                                      1   2   3   4   5   6   7   8   9   10
(verbal, emotional, physical, substance, alcohol)

_____

_____

Name: _____    Hector Suco    Date: _____

# Relationship Deal Breakers

Deal breakers are topics (potential) couples need to hash out before moving forward in their relationship. You may want to do this worksheet with your partner to spark a conversation. If you fill this out alone, you can use it to find out what you need from your other half before you start looking for a partner.

For #1 – 12, circle 1 – 10 based on how important each are in your life with 1 being the least important and 10 being extremely important. Then, write how important they are to you when it comes to your partner.

1. Having children                       1  2  3  4  5  6  7  8  9  10

_____

_____

2. How you raise your children           1  2  3  4  5  6  7  8  9  10

_____

_____

3. Life goals                            1  2  3  4  5  6  7  8  9  10

_____

_____

4. Religion                              1  2  3  4  5  6  7  8  9  10

_____

_____

5. Where to live or settle down          1  2  3  4  5  6  7  8  9  10

_____

_____

6. Finances                                   1   2   3   4   5   6   7   8   9   10

_____

_____

7. Taste in music, movies, TV                 1   2   3   4   5   6   7   8   9   10

_____

_____

8. Politics                                   1   2   3   4   5   6   7   8   9   10

_____

_____

9. Travel/Vacations                           1   2   3   4   5   6   7   8   9   10

_____

_____

10. Sex                                       1   2   3   4   5   6   7   8   9   10

_____

_____

11. Occupation                                1   2   3   4   5   6   7   8   9   10

_____

_____

12. Abuse                                     1   2   3   4   5   6   7   8   9   10
(verbal, emotional, physical, substance, alcohol)

_____

_____

Name: _____     Hector Suco     Date: _____

# Relationship Deal Breakers

Deal breakers are topics (potential) couples need to hash out before moving forward in their relationship. You may want to do this worksheet with your partner to spark a conversation. If you fill this out alone, you can use it to find out what you need from your other half before you start looking for a partner.

For #1 – 12, circle 1 – 10 based on how important each are in your life with 1 being the least important and 10 being extremely important. Then, write how important they are to you when it comes to your partner.

1. Having children                  1   2   3   4   5   6   7   8   9   10

_____

_____

2. How you raise your children       1   2   3   4   5   6   7   8   9   10

_____

_____

3. Life goals                         1   2   3   4   5   6   7   8   9   10

_____

_____

4. Religion                          1   2   3   4   5   6   7   8   9   10

_____

_____

5. Where to live or settle down       1   2   3   4   5   6   7   8   9   10

_____

_____

6. Finances                                      1  2  3  4  5  6  7  8  9  10

_____

_____

7. Taste in music, movies, TV          1  2  3  4  5  6  7  8  9  10

_____

_____

8. Politics                                       1  2  3  4  5  6  7  8  9  10

_____

_____

9. Travel/Vacations                          1  2  3  4  5  6  7  8  9  10

_____

_____

10. Sex                                              1  2  3  4  5  6  7  8  9  10

_____

_____

11. Occupation                                 1  2  3  4  5  6  7  8  9  10

_____

_____

12. Abuse                                         1  2  3  4  5  6  7  8  9  10
(verbal, emotional, physical, substance, alcohol)

_____

_____

# Relationship Deal Breakers Worksheet Guide

1. Having children is a common life goal. How many children do you want? How important is it for you to have biological children (flesh and blood)? If you or your partner are infertile, will you consider adoption? Would you be willing to try in vitro fertilization?

2. When a couple have children, they should come to an agreement as far as how to raise them, what schools to send them to, how much money to spend on them, what values to instill in them, or what, if any, religion will they be raised in. If religion is not important to you, how would you feel about raising your children in a religious environment due to your partner's beliefs?

3. You and your partner should have life's goals that are similar or able to come together without clashing. Whether it is having children, climbing Mount Everest, run a marathon, or traveling, you need to be able to live with, and ultimately support, each others' dreams

4. Although you shouldn't to bring it up on the first date, religion is important. Success stories of couples who practice different religions exist all over the world. These people see it as an obstacle, not a wall. How do you see it? How important is it that you date someone within your religion?

5. Location. Location. Location. How close is your family, where you work, and other factors determine where you and your partner will live. Would you stop dating someone, break off an engagement, or even divorce someone because their job is relocating or just because they want a change of scenery?

6. Some people like to save while others spend without a care. Would it bother you if your partner liked to gamble as a hobby? Would you mind if they started to lend money to friends without setting a date to be paid back by? Will you want a joint account or separate accounts? If the accounts are separate, how important will it be for you to see their spending habits?

7. It is unlikely that you and your partner will have the same tastes in everything. There are funny pictures online that say, "If your woman doesn't know what [insert common movie reference here] is, she's not the one!" But sometimes showing your partner new things turn out great. Even if you disagree on movies or music, take turns. Compromise is key.

8. Republican Mary Matalin and Democrat James Carville are happily married. They have been able to put their political ideals aside in the name of love. Would you be able to date someone who doesn't share your political views? Would you argue because of it?

9. Some people want to travel the world while others are perfectly content with staying around or at home. Some need to go somewhere new every time they venture out, and others have one favorite place they just cannot help but go back to. Where do you fall on the spectrum? What about your partner? Can you compromise?

10. How important is sex in your relationships? How often do you want to have sex? Are there certain things, likes or dislikes, that you or your partner just won't budge on? Can you respect that?

11. The issue may not be the occupation itself, but the pay and/or lifestyle. Would you be okay with someone that has a job that requires them to work at night and sleep during the day? Firefighters are gone for 24 to 48 hours at a time. Police officers put their life on the line every day. Are you okay with all jobs or are there some jobs you do not want your partner to have?

12. You need to be clear with your partner about what is acceptable and what is not. Physical, verbal, or psychological abuse should be a deal breaker in **any** type of relationship. Would you be okay with your partner taking drugs? Would you mind if they had a drink or two or three every day? How about smoking cigarettes?

The phrase "love conquers all" is not always applicable. Love cannot always combat problems within our relationships. Sometimes, unfortunately, love just is not enough. Be aware of what your preferences are so that you can share them with your partner. Remember, compromise and communication are key.

I hope this has helped you.
Good luck on your journey.

Name: _____  Hector Suco  Date: _____

# Friends With Benefits

1. Who is the person you have this friendship with? _____

2. How long has this relationship been going on? _____

3. If you are having sex, what type of protection are you using?

   _____

4. What would happen if a pregnancy occurs?

   _____

   _____

5. How long do you want this relationship to continue?

   _____

   _____

6. Friends with benefits are two people who are in a sexual relationship, but are not exclusive. Are you two exclusive?
   - ☐ Yes
   - ☐ No

7. What would happen if they become attracted to someone else?

   _____

   _____

8. How would you feel if someone else catches your friend's eye?

   _____

   _____

9. Do you ever see yourself actually dating this person?
   - ☐ Yes
   - ☐ No

10. Do you ever want something more?

_____

_____

11. If this relationship stops for whatever reason, would you want to stay friends?

_____

_____

Name: _____    Hector Suco    Date: _____

# Friends With Benefits

1. Who is the person you have this friendship with? _____

2. How long has this relationship been going on? _____

3. If you are having sex, what type of protection are you using?

_____

4. What would happen if a pregnancy occurs?

_____

_____

5. How long do you want this relationship to continue?

_____

_____

6. Friends with benefits are two people who are in a sexual relationship, but are not exclusive. Are you two exclusive?
  ☐ Yes    ☐ No

7. What would happen if they become attracted to someone else?

_____

_____

8. How would you feel if someone else catches your friend's eye?

_____

_____

9. Do you ever see yourself actually dating this person?
  ☐ Yes    ☐ No

10. Do you ever want something more?

_____

_____


11. If this relationship stops for whatever reason, would you want to stay friends?

_____

_____

Name: _____    Hector Suco    Date: _____

# Friends With Benefits

1. Who is the person you have this friendship with? _____

2. How long has this relationship been going on? _____

3. If you are having sex, what type of protection are you using?
   _____

4. What would happen if a pregnancy occurs?
   _____
   _____

5. How long do you want this relationship to continue?
   _____
   _____

6. Friends with benefits are two people who are in a sexual relationship, but are not exclusive. Are you two exclusive?
   ☐ Yes          ☐ No

7. What would happen if they become attracted to someone else?
   _____
   _____

8. How would you feel if someone else catches your friend's eye?
   _____
   _____

9. Do you ever see yourself actually dating this person?
   ☐ Yes          ☐ No

10. Do you ever want something more?

_____

_____

11. If this relationship stops for whatever reason, would you want to stay friends?

_____

_____

# Friends With Benefits Worksheet Guide

3. & 4. Your trust in your friend should not be a factor when it comes to sexually transmitted diseases and infections or when it comes to protection from a possible pregnancy, even if the chances are 99.9%. This is not something you should wait to talk about until it is happening.

5. Examples include:
- Indefinitely
- Until I find someone else
- Until x amount of time has passed because feelings can get involved
- Until it gets boring
- Until I get over my ex.

7. & 8. The amount or lack of emotional attachment will determine the answer to this question. Would it matter to you if your partner had a random fling with another person? Would it matter if they didn't tell you? In the reverse, would it matter to your partner if you had a random fling with another person? Would it matter if you do not tell them? Do you have to mention if that happens to one another?

9. How easy will it be to let go of this arrangement?

10. Do you want something more out of this relationship? Do you know how your partner feels about it? Do you fear that they won't want to continue if you tell them?

11. If there was truly no emotional attachment, you could hypothetically stay as friends. Just be honest with yourself.

I hope this has helped you.
Good luck on your journey.

Name: _____     Hector Suco     Date: _____

# Dating

1. What is your relationship status? (Select one)

|   | **Status** | **Definition** | **Go To:** |
|---|---|---|---|
| ☐ | Talking to multiple people | Dating more than one person, multiple times each | Question #2, Stop at #18 |
| ☐ | Talking to someone | Going on dates with the same person for a short period of time | |
| ☐ | Talking to 2 people | Dating 2 people, multiple times each. | Question #3, Skip #19 |
| ☐ | Dating Scene | Dating multiple people mostly once, maybe twice | |
| ☐ | Exclusive | Dating same person and no one else | Question #3, Stop at #19 |

2. How do you search for someone to date? (Select all that apply)

☐ Friends  ☐ Online  ☐ Outings  ☐ Hookups/Blind Dates

☐ Speed Dating

3. What is your **ultimate goal** when dating? (Select one)

☐ Love/Marriage/Family   ☐ Sex   ☐ Companionship

☐ Other: _____

For #4 – 18, circle 1 – 10 based on how important each is when looking for a potential partner with 1 being the least important to 10 being very important. Then, write why you circled that number. Give specifics reasons.
Also, look at how the person you're dating in comparison to these factors.

4. Age     1   2   3   4   5   6   7   8   9   10

___

5. Race     1   2   3   4   5   6   7   8   9   10

___

6. Religion     1   2   3   4   5   6   7   8   9   10

___

7. Location     1   2   3   4   5   6   7   8   9   10

___

8. Income     1   2   3   4   5   6   7   8   9   10

___

9. Profession     1   2   3   4   5   6   7   8   9   10

___

10. Interests     1   2   3   4   5   6   7   8   9   10

___

11. Past Relationships/Marriage     1   2   3   4   5   6   7   8   9   10

___

12. Children (Existing & Future)     1   2   3   4   5   6   7   8   9   10

___

13. Dominance/Recessive          1   2   3   4   5   6   7   8   9   10

_____

14. Confidence                   1   2   3   4   5   6   7   8   9   10

_____

15. Argumentative                1   2   3   4   5   6   7   8   9   10

_____

16. Affectionate                 1   2   3   4   5   6   7   8   9   10

_____

17. Intelligence                 1   2   3   4   5   6   7   8   9   10

_____

18. Looks                        1   2   3   4   5   6   7   8   9   10

_____

19. Do you want to take this relationship to the next level?

☐ Yes (Go to #19A)    ☐ No (Go to #19D)    ☐ I do not know (Go to #19E)

19A. Have you told them?    ☐ Yes (Go to #19B)    ☐ No (Go to #19C)

19B. What did they say? _____

_____

19C. Why not? _____

_____

19D. Do you know if they want to take the relationship to the next level?

☐ Yes            ☐ No

19E. Below, list your partner's positive and negative attributes and compare them. Then, describe how you think life will be like in the future with and without this person in your life. After, decide if you want to stay where you are or take the relationship to the next level.

| Positive Attributes: | Negative Attributes: |
|---|---|
|  |  |
|  |  |
|  |  |
|  |  |
|  |  |
| Describe what life will be like in the future ||
| … with them. | … without them. |
|  |  |
|  |  |
|  |  |
|  |  |

20. Are you trying to pick between two people?
- ☐ Yes (Continue below)
- ☐ No (Stop here)

| Name: _____ || Name: _____ ||
|---|---|---|---|
| Positive Attributes: | Negative Attributes: | Positive Attributes: | Negative Attributes: |
|  |  |  |  |
|  |  |  |  |
|  |  |  |  |
|  |  |  |  |
| Describe how life will be like **with each** in the future. ||||
|  |  |  |  |
|  |  |  |  |
|  |  |  |  |
|  |  |  |  |
|  |  |  |  |
|  |  |  |  |

Name: _____   Hector Suco   Date: _____

# Dating

1. What is your relationship status? (Select one)

|   | Status | Definition | Go To: |
|---|---|---|---|
| ☐ | Talking to multiple people | Dating more than one person, multiple times each | Question #2, Stop at #18 |
| ☐ | Talking to someone | Going on dates with the same person for a short period of time | |
| ☐ | Talking to 2 people | Dating 2 people, multiple times each. | Question #3, Skip #19 |
| ☐ | Dating Scene | Dating multiple people mostly once, maybe twice | |
| ☐ | Exclusive | Dating same person and no one else | Question #3, Stop at #19 |

2. How do you search for someone to date? (Select all that apply)

☐ Friends  ☐ Online  ☐ Outings  ☐ Hookups/Blind Dates

☐ Speed Dating

3. What is your **ultimate goal** when dating? (Select one)

☐ Love/Marriage/Family   ☐ Sex   ☐ Companionship

☐ Other: _____

For #4 – 18, circle 1 – 10 based on how important each is when looking for a potential partner with 1 being the least important to 10 being very important. Then, write why you circled that number. Give specifics reasons.
Also, look at how the person you're dating in comparison to these factors.

4. Age                               1    2    3    4    5    6    7    8    9    10

_____

5. Race                              1    2    3    4    5    6    7    8    9    10

_____

6. Religion                      1    2    3    4    5    6    7    8    9    10

_____

7. Location                    1    2    3    4    5    6    7    8    9    10

_____

8. Income                     1    2    3    4    5    6    7    8    9    10

_____

9. Profession                1    2    3    4    5    6    7    8    9    10

_____

10. Interests                1    2    3    4    5    6    7    8    9    10

_____

11. Past Relationships/Marriage   1    2    3    4    5    6    7    8    9    10

_____

12. Children (Existing & Future)    1    2    3    4    5    6    7    8    9    10

_____

13. Dominance/Recessive        1   2   3   4   5   6   7   8   9   10

14. Confidence                 1   2   3   4   5   6   7   8   9   10

15. Argumentative              1   2   3   4   5   6   7   8   9   10

16. Affectionate               1   2   3   4   5   6   7   8   9   10

17. Intelligence               1   2   3   4   5   6   7   8   9   10

18. Looks                      1   2   3   4   5   6   7   8   9   10

19. Do you want to take this relationship to the next level?

☐ Yes (Go to #19A)    ☐ No (Go to #19D)    ☐ I do not know (Go to #19E)

19A. Have you told them?   ☐ Yes (Go to #19B)   ☐ No (Go to #19C)

19B. What did they say? _____

19C. Why not? _____

19D. Do you know if they want to take the relationship to the next level?

☐ Yes          ☐ No

19E. Below, list your partner's positive and negative attributes and compare them. Then, describe how you think life will be like in the future with and without this person in your life. After, decide if you want to stay where you are or take the relationship to the next level.

| Positive Attributes: | Negative Attributes: |
|---|---|
|  |  |
|  |  |
|  |  |
|  |  |
|  |  |
| Describe what life will be like in the future ||
| … with them. | … without them. |
|  |  |
|  |  |
|  |  |
|  |  |
|  |  |

20. Are you trying to pick between two people?
- ☐ Yes (Continue below)
- ☐ No (Stop here)

| Name: _____ || Name: _____ ||
|---|---|---|---|
| Positive Attributes: | Negative Attributes: | Positive Attributes: | Negative Attributes: |
|  |  |  |  |
|  |  |  |  |
|  |  |  |  |
|  |  |  |  |
|  |  |  |  |
| Describe how life will be like **with each** in the future. ||||
|  |  |  |  |
|  |  |  |  |
|  |  |  |  |
|  |  |  |  |
|  |  |  |  |
|  |  |  |  |

Name: _____   Hector Suco   Date: _____

# Dating

1. What is your relationship status? (Select one)

|   | **Status** | **Definition** | **Go To:** |
|---|---|---|---|
| ☐ | Talking to multiple people | Dating more than one person, multiple times each | Question #2, Stop at #18 |
| ☐ | Talking to someone | Going on dates with the same person for a short period of time | |
| ☐ | Talking to 2 people | Dating 2 people, multiple times each. | Question #3, Skip #19 |
| ☐ | Dating Scene | Dating multiple people mostly once, maybe twice | |
| ☐ | Exclusive | Dating same person and no one else | Question #3, Stop at #19 |

2. How do you search for someone to date? (Select all that apply)

☐ Friends    ☐ Online   ☐ Outings    ☐ Hookups/Blind Dates

☐ Speed Dating

3. What is your **ultimate goal** when dating? (Select one)

☐ Love/Marriage/Family    ☐ Sex    ☐ Companionship

☐ Other: _____

For #4 – 18, circle 1 – 10 based on how important each is when looking for a potential partner with 1 being the least important to 10 being very important. Then, write why you circled that number. Give specifics reasons.
Also, look at how the person you're dating in comparison to these factors.

4. Age        1 2 3 4 5 6 7 8 9 10

_____

5. Race        1 2 3 4 5 6 7 8 9 10

_____

6. Religion       1 2 3 4 5 6 7 8 9 10

_____

7. Location       1 2 3 4 5 6 7 8 9 10

_____

8. Income       1 2 3 4 5 6 7 8 9 10

_____

9. Profession      1 2 3 4 5 6 7 8 9 10

_____

10. Interests       1 2 3 4 5 6 7 8 9 10

_____

11. Past Relationships/Marriage 1 2 3 4 5 6 7 8 9 10

_____

12. Children (Existing & Future) 1 2 3 4 5 6 7 8 9 10

_____

13. Dominance/Recessive        1  2  3  4  5  6  7  8  9  10

14. Confidence                 1  2  3  4  5  6  7  8  9  10

15. Argumentative              1  2  3  4  5  6  7  8  9  10

16. Affectionate               1  2  3  4  5  6  7  8  9  10

17. Intelligence               1  2  3  4  5  6  7  8  9  10

18. Looks                      1  2  3  4  5  6  7  8  9  10

19. Do you want to take this relationship to the next level?

☐ Yes (Go to #19A)    ☐ No (Go to #19D)    ☐ I do not know (Go to #19E)

19A. Have you told them?   ☐ Yes (Go to #19B)   ☐ No (Go to #19C)

19B. What did they say? _____

_____

19C. Why not? _____

_____

19D. Do you know if they want to take the relationship to the next level?

☐ Yes          ☐ No

19E. Below, list your partner's positive and negative attributes and compare them. Then, describe how you think life will be like in the future with and without this person in your life. After, decide if you want to stay where you are or take the relationship to the next level.

| Positive Attributes: | Negative Attributes: |
|---|---|
|  |  |
|  |  |
|  |  |
|  |  |
|  |  |
| Describe what life will be like in the future ||
| … with them. | … without them. |
|  |  |
|  |  |
|  |  |
|  |  |

20. Are you trying to pick between two people?
    ☐ Yes (Continue below)
    ☐ No (Stop here)

| Name: _____ || Name: _____ ||
|---|---|---|---|
| Positive Attributes: | Negative Attributes: | Positive Attributes: | Negative Attributes: |
|  |  |  |  |
|  |  |  |  |
|  |  |  |  |
|  |  |  |  |
| Describe how life will be like **with each** in the future. ||||
|  |  |  |  |
|  |  |  |  |
|  |  |  |  |
|  |  |  |  |
|  |  |  |  |
|  |  |  |  |

# Dating Worksheet Guide

1. Everyone, including companies, have a different set of "relationship statuses," from Facebook to eHarmony. Try to "define" your relationship in the best way you can. If more than one match, follow both sets of instructions next to the questions.

2. Online: According to nasdaq.com, in 2015, Americans spent an estimated $2 billion on online dating sites. People go out of their way to try to find that special someone, but you shouldn't live beyond your means. Make sure you keep your budget in mind as you explore the dating scene.

3. People go on dates for different reasons. Some people might not be looking for the choices listed in the worksheet. They may just go out to have a good time. Young adults might be looking for "true love." Some people search for companionship if they do not necessarily want to start a family or do not believe in marriage.

4. Consider your own age when deciding your age range when dating. Some people want to date older people due to maturity and experience. Others will want to date younger people because of their energy and vibrancy. While many pick an age range closer to their own age, and others will tell you that dating someone even ten years younger or older than you is normal. As long as no one is breaking any laws, age is just a number.

5. Race is a social construct, but has some backing by science. Out of 80,000 genes in the human genome, about 320 genes separate one race over another. Your idea of what race to date may come from your own view or it may be formed through your interactions with family, friends, and what you think society expects of you, but decide for yourself and not other people.

6. Religion is an important part of many people's lives. It dictates their values and moral compasses. So, to answer this question, you first need to determine how important religion is in your life. Would you ever compromise some or any part of your religious affiliations for your partner?

7. Are you okay with long distance relationships? Are you okay with your date/partner being an hour drive from you? How close or far away do they need to be?

8. Would you date someone who is making minimum wage? Is there a minimum salary that your potential partner needs to have in order for them to be eligible? There is not anything wrong with wanting to be financially stable, but try not to let this be your main criteria.

9. Are there professions that you do not wish your potential partner to have? Would you be okay dating someone who needs to put their life on the line everyday like police officers, firefighters, or military personnel? What if they had no profession? What if they wanted to be a stay-at-home parent?

10. Do you need to share many interests?

11. Past relationships are often times referred to "baggage." The mark of a good partner is someone who is willing to open that baggage up and sort it with you. How much are you willing to help your partner sort through?

12. Children, existing and future, should always be talked about within the first month or so of dating. Postponing this conversation may only lead to confusion later on. However, the importance of having new or more children can be discussed at a later date.

13. When it comes to any kind of relationship, there is a yin and a yang. Do you want a "more dominant" partner to take care of you and make decisions? Do you need to be the dominant partner? Try to find balance in your relationships.

14. Confidence is important. What levels of confidence are you okay with and not okay with? Is someone without confidence a turn off for you?

15. The perfect couple does not exist. There will be disagreements.

16. Are you a touchy-feely person? How do you feel about public displays of affection?

17. Is intelligence level important to you? Do you and your friends like to have intelligent discussions? Do you need your partner to keep up with you? Do you need to be able to keep up with them?

18. Do you need to be immediately attracted to your partner, or do you believe that physical attraction can be built over time? How important is the way they look?

19. Be honest with yourself with these questions.

20. Yes: You will have to wrestle with your emotions and ultimately choose one person that will make you happy. Try not to settle and make sure you let all parties involved know you decide. No one wants to be strung along.

I hope this has helped you.
Good luck on your journey.

Name: _____   Hector Suco   Date: _____

# In A Relationship

This worksheet can be filled out by you alone or with your partner. It is up to your discretion.

1. How long have you been in your relationship? _____

2. How would you rate your relationship?

```
|—————————————————|—————————————————|
0                 5                 10
```

3. Why did you give your relationship that rating?

_____

_____

4. How can you improve your relationship?

_____

_____

5. What are some of your goals as a couple?

_____

_____

_____

6. Have you ever been romantically attracted to someone else while in your current relationship? If so, explain.

_____

_____

7. Have you ever been tempted by someone else to betray/cheat on your partner?

_____

_____

8. Have you ever betrayed/cheated on your partner? Has your partner ever betrayed/cheated on you?

_____

_____

_____

_____

# Finances

9. Which describes your bank account(s)?
   ☐ Joint Account
   ☐ Separate Accounts
   ☐ Both Joint & Separate Accounts

9A: Do you have a secret bank account that your partner does not know about?
   ☐ No
   ☐ Yes: Explain: _____

10. Have you and/or your partner ever over drafted? If so, why?

_____

_____

11. Do you and/or your partner have savings or investment accounts? Explain.

_____

_____

12. Do you and/or your partner have debt? How much? How are you handling your debt?

_____

_____

13. What are your financial goals as a couple?

_____

_____

# Children

14. Do you have children?
- ☐ No
- ☐ Yes: How many?_____ How old are they?_____
   If your children are over 18, are they still living at home? _____

15. Do you want (more) children?
- ☐ No
- ☐ Yes: How many (more)?_____ By when? _____

# Social Life

16. How would you describe your social life with your partner?

_____

_____

17. How often do you go out with other friends without your partner?

_____

_____

18. Are there any hobbies you share and practice with your partner?

_____

_____

# Religion

19. What religion do you and your partner practice?

_____

_____

20. How important is religion in your relationship?

_____

_____

# Sex

21. Are you and your partner intimate (having sex)?
- ☐ Yes (Skip 22)
- ☐ No (Skip 23 & 24)

22. When or how long from now are you planning on being intimate?

_____

23. How often do you have sex? _____

24. Are you content with your sex life?
- ☐ Yes
- ☐ No: Why not?

_____

_____

# Values

For #25 – 33, choose 1 – 10 based on how important each is in your relationship with 1 being the least important to 10 being the most important. Then, write how important they are to you when it comes to your partner.

25. Respect, Honesty & Trust        1  2  3  4  5  6  7  8  9  10

_____

_____

26. Life Goals, Lifestyle           1  2  3  4  5  6  7  8  9  10

_____

_____

27. Career                          1  2  3  4  5  6  7  8  9  10

_____

_____

28. Religion                        1  2  3  4  5  6  7  8  9  10

_____

_____

29. Commitment/Loyalty              1  2  3  4  5  6  7  8  9  10

_____

_____

30. Selflessness/Sacrifice        1   2   3   4   5   6   7   8   9   10

_____

_____

31. Patience/Forgiveness          1   2   3   4   5   6   7   8   9   10

_____

_____

32. Children                      1   2   3   4   5   6   7   8   9   10

_____

_____

33. Family                        1   2   3   4   5   6   7   8   9   10

_____

_____

Name: _____   Hector Suco   Date: _____

# In A Relationship

This worksheet can be filled out by you alone or with your partner. It is up to your discretion.

1. How long have you been in your relationship? _____

2. How would you rate your relationship?

```
|――――――――――――――|――――――――――――――――――――――――|
0              5                         10
```

3. Why did you give your relationship that rating?

_____

_____

4. How can you improve your relationship?

_____

_____

5. What are some of your goals as a couple?

_____

_____

_____

6. Have you ever been romantically attracted to someone else while in your current relationship? If so, explain.

_____

_____

7. Have you ever been tempted by someone else to betray/cheat on your partner?

_____

_____

8. Have you ever betrayed/cheated on your partner? Has your partner ever betrayed/cheated on you?

_____

_____

_____

_____

# Finances

9. Which describes your bank account(s)?
- ☐ Joint Account
- ☐ Separate Accounts
- ☐ Both Joint & Separate Accounts

9A: Do you have a secret bank account that your partner does not know about?
- ☐ No
- ☐ Yes: Explain: _____

10. Have you and/or your partner ever over drafted? If so, why?

_____

_____

11. Do you and/or your partner have savings or investment accounts? Explain.

_____

_____

12. Do you and/or your partner have debt? How much? How are you handling your debt?

_____

_____

13. What are your financial goals as a couple?

_____

_____

# Children

14. Do you have children?
☐  No
☐  Yes: How many?_____ How old are they?_____
If your children are over 18, are they still living at home? _____

15. Do you want (more) children?
☐  No
☐  Yes: How many (more)?_____ By when? _____

# Social Life

16. How would you describe your social life with your partner?

_____

_____

17. How often do you go out with other friends without your partner?

_____

_____

18. Are there any hobbies you share and practice with your partner?

_____

_____

# Religion

19. What religion do you and your partner practice?

_____

_____

20. How important is religion in your relationship?

_____

_____

# Sex

21. Are you and your partner intimate (having sex)?
- ☐ Yes (Skip 22)
- ☐ No (Skip 23 & 24)

22. When or how long from now are you planning on being intimate?

_____

23. How often do you have sex? _____

24. Are you content with your sex life?
- ☐ Yes
- ☐ No: Why not?

_____

_____

# Values

For #25 – 33, choose 1 – 10 based on how important each is in your relationship with 1 being the least important to 10 being the most important. Then, write how important they are to you when it comes to your partner.

25. Respect, Honesty & Trust      1   2   3   4   5   6   7   8   9   10

_____

_____

26. Life Goals, Lifestyle      1   2   3   4   5   6   7   8   9   10

_____

_____

27. Career      1   2   3   4   5   6   7   8   9   10

_____

_____

28. Religion      1   2   3   4   5   6   7   8   9   10

_____

_____

29. Commitment/Loyalty      1   2   3   4   5   6   7   8   9   10

_____

_____

30. Selflessness/Sacrifice		1	2	3	4	5	6	7	8	9	10

_____

_____

31. Patience/Forgiveness		1	2	3	4	5	6	7	8	9	10

_____

_____

32. Children		1	2	3	4	5	6	7	8	9	10

_____

_____

33. Family		1	2	3	4	5	6	7	8	9	10

_____

_____

Name: _____    Hector Suco    Date: _____

# In A Relationship

This worksheet can be filled out by you alone or with your partner. It is up to your discretion.

1. How long have you been in your relationship? _____

2. How would you rate your relationship?

```
+----------------+----------------+
0                5                10
```

3. Why did you give your relationship that rating?

_____

_____

4. How can you improve your relationship?

_____

_____

5. What are some of your goals as a couple?

_____

_____

_____

6. Have you ever been romantically attracted to someone else while in your current relationship? If so, explain.

_____

_____

7. Have you ever been tempted by someone else to betray/cheat on your partner?

_____

_____

8. Have you ever betrayed/cheated on your partner? Has your partner ever betrayed/cheated on you?

_____

_____

_____

_____

# Finances

9. Which describes your bank account(s)?
   - ☐ Joint Account
   - ☐ Separate Accounts
   - ☐ Both Joint & Separate Accounts

9A: Do you have a secret bank account that your partner does not know about?
   - ☐ No
   - ☐ Yes: Explain: _____

10. Have you and/or your partner ever over drafted? If so, why?

_____

_____

11. Do you and/or your partner have savings or investment accounts? Explain.

_____

_____

12. Do you and/or your partner have debt? How much? How are you handling your debt?

_____

_____

13. What are your financial goals as a couple?

_____

_____

# Children

14. Do you have children?
- ☐ No
- ☐ Yes: How many?_____ How old are they?_____
   If your children are over 18, are they still living at home? _____

15. Do you want (more) children?
- ☐ No
- ☐ Yes: How many (more)?_____ By when? _____

# Social Life

16. How would you describe your social life with your partner?

_____

_____

17. How often do you go out with other friends without your partner?

_____

_____

18. Are there any hobbies you share and practice with your partner?

_____

_____

# Religion

19. What religion do you and your partner practice?

_____

_____

20. How important is religion in your relationship?

_____

_____

# Sex

21. Are you and your partner intimate (having sex)?
    - ☐ Yes (Skip 22)
    - ☐ No (Skip 23 & 24)

22. When or how long from now are you planning on being intimate?

_____

23. How often do you have sex? _____

24. Are you content with your sex life?
    - ☐ Yes
    - ☐ No: Why not?

_____

_____

# Values

For #25 – 33, choose 1 – 10 based on how important each is in your relationship with 1 being the least important to 10 being the most important. Then, write how important they are to you when it comes to your partner.

25. Respect, Honesty & Trust          1  2  3  4  5  6  7  8  9  10

_____

_____

26. Life Goals, Lifestyle              1  2  3  4  5  6  7  8  9  10

_____

_____

27. Career                             1  2  3  4  5  6  7  8  9  10

_____

_____

28. Religion                           1  2  3  4  5  6  7  8  9  10

_____

_____

29. Commitment/Loyalty                 1  2  3  4  5  6  7  8  9  10

_____

_____

30. Selflessness/Sacrifice		1  2  3  4  5  6  7  8  9  10

_____

_____

31. Patience/Forgiveness		1  2  3  4  5  6  7  8  9  10

_____

_____

32. Children				1  2  3  4  5  6  7  8  9  10

_____

_____

33. Family				1  2  3  4  5  6  7  8  9  10

_____

_____

# In A Relationship Worksheet Guide

2. Your answers will differ throughout your life. Relationships have their ups and downs. If your partner were to answer this question in secret, would your answers match?

3. Rating of 1-3: Write down your problems, no matter how big or small. What needs the most work and how are the both of you going to bring that number up?

Rating of 4-8: Your relationship is good, but it could be better. Write down the good and the bad. What is working and not working in your relationship. How can it be better?

Rating of 9: Excellent. Write down what you think is stopping your relationship from becoming a 10.

Rating of 10: Congratulations on being so happy! So many people aspire to be where you are. Keep it up!

4. No relationship is perfect. Whether it is something big or something that seems unimportant, write how you think your relationship can be improved. Do not just write how much your partner needs to change. You will have to make adjustments as well if you want your relationship to work. How you do that is up to you both.

5. Examples include:

| Better/More Sex | Better/More Communication | Get out of debt | Have a better social life | Have children |
|---|---|---|---|---|
| Try new activities together | Go on more dates | Save more money | Say "I love you" more often | Spend more quality time together as a family |
| Work less | More time alone together | Add more romance | Share chores | Share more non- sexual intimacy |

6. Feeling physically attracted to someone else is natural. However, this may suggest a deeper issue: a lessening commitment to your partner. Your partner should be your number one.

7. Anyone can be tempted to cheat on/betray his or her partner. It could start with a friendly hug, or casual glance. These things can mimic intimacy. If it does happen, trust yourself to notice and remember the promises you made to your partner.

8. Please use the Romantic Betrayed or Romantic Betrayer Worksheet.

9. Having a joint account or separate accounts is a decision all couples need to think about. If a couple is on the fence about which account(s) to have, they should seek out a financial advisor.

9A. I believe honesty is the best policy. You could be working a side job to earn some extra money for spending, or even to buy your partner a gift. However, if your partner finds out that the account has been hidden from them, then it will most likely cause distrust. You could have an account that neither of you can touch for a certain amount of time or unless it is for a certain purpose, but there is not any good reason for a secret account.

10. Over-drafting a bank account is never fun, especially when the fee hits. You and your partner should be open about your spending, especially if you share an account or accounts. You should work as a team to make sure you're always got a few dollars to spare, just in case.

11. Examples of savings accounts include:

| Emergency | Vacation | Children | Projects |
|---|---|---|---|
| House Expenses | Car Expenses | Retirement | Hobbies |

Go see a financial advisor to start investing.

12. Debt is a part of life, but it does not have to be a dark cloud hanging over you. There are many ways to free yourself from debt such as debt stacking, using a debt-relief program, or consolidating your debt into one payment through a debt consolidation company. Use a financial advisor as needed.

13. Examples include:

| Get out of / Lower debt | Invest (more) | Save money | Create an Emergency Fund |
|---|---|---|---|

14. What role do your children play in your relationship? Do they enhance your relationship? Does taking care of them leave you short on time or energy for your partner?

15. Are you ready to take on the responsibilities of being a parent? Are you emotionally and financially ready to have a child, or another child?

16. Being social is a healthy part of being a well-rounded individual. A night out on the town, going to a nice restaurant, a game night with friends, a sports event, going to a concert, etc. These all help keep you young, feeling alive, and happy.

17. Not all partners are okay with a girls-night-out or guys-night-out. If this is the case, there may be some trust issues. Being okay with your partner going out without you means (and shows them) that you trust them.

18. Having common hobbies is always a plus. If you do not share any hobbies, try to find one!

19. Do you and your partner practice the same religion? Different religions? Do you or your partner not practice religion at all? If you and your partner do not practice the same religion, how do you celebrate the holidays? If marriage and children is the end goal for you, or if you already have children, have you talked about which religion you will raise your children in?

20. If you and your partner have the same answer, this is excellent. Having almost the same answer is good too. If you and your partner have different answers, sit down and discuss it. If religion is essential to one of you, the other should be willing to understand that.

21. Married or not, sex and intimacy (or lack there of) are very important aspects of a romantic partnership. Personal, religious, and cultural values are in play. Ask your partner how they feel about becoming intimate if you are not already. Before you and your partner decide to become intimate, decide on which form of protection to choose to prevent pregnancy, unless you both decide you want children. Make sure you have some idea of what you're getting into, and try to secure your finances as much as you possibly can. Do some research and make the right decision for you, your partner, and (any possible) future children.

22. Examples include:

| After we've been together for_____/ | When I'm ready | Waiting for marriage | I have to be sure that they won't dump me if and when we have sex. |
|---|---|---|---|
| Soon | When they are ready | I do not know | |

23. This number depends on each relationship. For some relationships, it is daily. For other relationships, it is weekly or maybe even monthly. As long as both partners are happy with what's going on, then the number doesn't actually matter. Besides, you and your partner should be the only people who actually know it.

24. If you are not happy with your sex life, write down why and how would you like your sex life to improve. "Having sex more often" is one answer, but what does that entail? What else needs to happen for the both of you to have sex more often? What gets your partner in the mood? Are children an obstacle to overcome? If the amount is not the issue, try to find the solutions that will work for you both.

25. What does being respected mean to you? Do you need that in a relationship? How honest do you expect each other to be? How upset would you be if you found out your partner lied? What if it was only a white lie?

26. You and your partner need to respect (and hopefully share) each other's life goals. Whether it is to have children, climb Mount Everest, or run a marathon, the respect and support needs to be there.

27. The issue may not be the occupation itself, but the pay and/or lifestyle. Would you be okay with someone that has a job that requires them to work at night and sleep during the day? Firefighters are gone for 24 to 48 hours at a time. Police officers put their life on the line every day. Would you be able to handle the difference in schedule?

28. Success stories of couples from different religions exist all over the world. If marriage is the goal, are you planning to get married with or without a religious affiliation? How important is religion in your relationship? Do you pray together? Apart? If you plan to have children, do you and/or your partner want to raise them to have a certain faith?

29. How do you define commitment? What about loyalty? Does that entail monogamy? Does it mean your partner must be 100% transparent? How important are promises? What happens if a promise between you and your partner is broken?

30. How much do you feel your partner should "sacrifice" for you in your relationship? How much do you feel you should? What can or cannot be given up?

31. Renowned novelist and lyricist Paulo Coelho mused that patience is so important because it makes us pay attention. Take the time to figure things out with your partner - dedicate yourself to trying to make things better. Listen and observe.

"Patience is bitter, but its fruit is sweet."
-Aristotle.

32. How important are children (or not having children)? How does your partner feel?

33. Do you believe in "family over everything"? Do you have extended family that is involved in your life? Do you want them to be a part of your children's lives?

I hope this has helped you.
Good luck on your journey.

Name: _____  Hector Suco  Date: _____

# Open Relationship

This worksheet can be filled out by you alone or with your partner(s). It is up to you.

1. How would you classify your relationship?

☐ One Partner        ☐ Open

2. How do you feel about being in an open relationship?

_____

_____

3. How do you think your partner feels about it?

_____

_____

4. Who suggested the open relationship?
☐ You (Go to #4A)
☐ Mutual suggestion (Go to #4B)
☐ We haven't talked about it (Go to #4C)

4A. Have you already introduced someone into your relationship? How did it happen? How did the introduction go?

_____

_____

4B. Where did the idea of an open relationship initially come from?

_____

_____

4C. How are you going to start the conversation?

_____

_____

5. What do you feel constitutes being "intimate" with another person?

_____

_____

6. How many people are you actively affectionate/intimate with?

☐  1 (Go to #7)          ☐  2 or more (Go to #6A)

6A. Do you live with any of them?
☐  Yes, I live with one of them (Go to #6B)
☐  Yes, I live with them (Go to #7)
☐  No (Go to #6B)

6B. Do they know each other?

☐  Yes (Go to #7)          ☐  No (Go to #6C)

6C. Are they aware of each other's presence in your life?

☐  Yes (Go to #7)          ☐  No (Go to #6D)

6D. How do you think your partner will react if they were to find out?

_____

_____

7. Do you or your partner have a prior relationship with the person entering your relationship?

_____

_____

8. How would you rate your relationship(s) from 1 - 10?

```
<----|------------------------|------------------------|---->
     0                        5                        10
```

Rating of 1-4: Explicitly write down your problems from the biggest to the smallest. What needs the most work and how are both of you going to bring this number up?

_____

_____

Rating of 5-7: An average relationship is okay, but it could be better. Write down the good and the bad. What is working and not working in your relationship. How can it be better?

_____

_____

Rating of 8-9: Excellent. Write down what is working. Also, write down the issues that are stopping your relationship from becoming a 10.

_____

_____

Rating of 10: Excellent job. Keep up the good work!

9. What are the boundaries you have set up for this new aspect of your relationship? (If you need more space, feel free to use another sheet of paper.)

_____

_____

_____

10. What will happen if one of you does not respect these boundaries?

_____

_____

11. Have expectations not been met in your relationship before? What was the outcome?

_____

_____

12. How often do you and your partner communicate with each other about feelings you may have for other people?

_____

_____

13. How would you react if your partner suggested being in a traditional relationship?

_____

_____

14. How would your partner react if you suggested being in a traditional relationship?

_____

_____

Name: _____  Hector Suco  Date: _____

# Open Relationship

This worksheet can be filled out by you alone or with your partner(s). It is up to you.

1. How would you classify your relationship?

☐   One Partner             ☐   Open

2. How do you feel about being in an open relationship?

_____

_____

3. How do you think your partner feels about it?

_____

_____

4. Who suggested the open relationship?
☐   You (Go to #4A)
☐   Mutual suggestion (Go to #4B)
☐   We haven't talked about it (Go to #4C)

4A. Have you already introduced someone into your relationship? How did it happen? How did the introduction go?

_____

_____

4B. Where did the idea of an open relationship initially come from?

_____

_____

4C. How are you going to start the conversation?

_____

_____

5. What do you feel constitutes being "intimate" with another person?

_____

_____

6. How many people are you actively affectionate/intimate with?

☐ 1 (Go to #7)   ☐ 2 or more (Go to #6A)

6A. Do you live with any of them?
☐ Yes, I live with one of them (Go to #6B)
☐ Yes, I live with them (Go to #7)
☐ No (Go to #6B)

6B. Do they know each other?

☐ Yes (Go to #7)   ☐ No (Go to #6C)

6C. Are they aware of each other's presence in your life?

☐ Yes (Go to #7)   ☐ No (Go to #6D)

6D. How do you think your partner will react if they were to find out?

_____

_____

7. Do you or your partner have a prior relationship with the person entering your relationship?

_____

_____

8. How would you rate your relationship(s) from 1 - 10?

```
0          5          10
```

Rating of 1-4: Explicitly write down your problems from the biggest to the smallest. What needs the most work and how are both of you going to bring this number up?

_____

_____

Rating of 5-7: An average relationship is okay, but it could be better. Write down the good and the bad. What is working and not working in your relationship. How can it be better?

_____

_____

Rating of 8-9: Excellent. Write down what is working. Also, write down the issues that are stopping your relationship from becoming a 10.

_____

_____

Rating of 10: Excellent job. Keep up the good work!

9. What are the boundaries you have set up for this new aspect of your relationship? (If you need more space, feel free to use another sheet of paper.)

_____

_____

_____

10. What will happen if one of you does not respect these boundaries?

_____

_____

11. Have expectations not been met in your relationship before? What was the outcome?

_____

_____

12. How often do you and your partner communicate with each other about feelings you may have for other people?

_____

_____

13. How would you react if your partner suggested being in a traditional relationship?

_____

_____

14. How would your partner react if you suggested being in a traditional relationship?

_____

_____

# Open Relationship Worksheet Guide

2. "Open" can mean many things. It can mean that you and your partner are able to be affectionate and intimate with other people outside of your unit. It can also mean that you two are open to sharing your bed (having sex) with other people. What does it mean to you? How would you feel about your relationship being this way?

3. Ask your partner what they think an open relationship is and find out their opinion on being in one.

4. Two people do not just expel the same idea at the same time. Someone must have said it first, even if you both believe in open relationships.

5. Some people think kissing is intimate; others do not, or base their opinion on the intentions behind a kiss. Figure out what you think does and does not constitute intimacy – think of things you may do with your partner that you do not do with other people.

6. This line of questioning is to make sure there are no secrets being held between you and your partner(s).

7. Do you know this person? Does your partner? Have one of you dated and/or been intimate with them before suggesting they become a part of your current relationship?

9. Do you both have the same boundaries? Is one more relaxed with the limitations than the other? How often do you communicate about these boundaries? Have they changed, become stricter, become more relaxed overtime? Do you have strict guidelines when it comes to flirting, kissing, touching, and/or sex with other people? Without communicating with you, are some more accepted than others? Do you expect your partner to tell you if anything happened between them and someone else?

10. What are the consequences for breaking any of these boundaries? How much of a role does forgiveness play in your relationship?

11. Describe, if anything, what has happened in your relationship before. This is not meant to relive your negative experiences, it is meant to learn from them.

12. If you see someone attractive, are you able to just tell that to your partner? Can they do the same? How about if you start to like someone as more than just a friend? Can you tell your partner without being scared of their reaction? Can they do the same?

13. & 14. I do not know what I would say if my wife asked me to be in an open relationship. It would take a lot of reflection and communication before giving an answer. That being said, transitioning from an open relationship to a more traditional one might require the same amount of thought and reflection, if not more. Think on how you would react to this type of change.

I hope this has helped you.
Good luck on your journey.

Name: _____   Hector Suco   Date: _____

# Love

This worksheet is for anyone currently in a romantic relationship.

1. What do you think love is? (Select all that apply)
   ☐ Feeling
   ☐ State of Mind
   ☐ Attitude
   ☐ Decision
   ☐ Other: _____

2. How much do you love yourself?

   ←|―――――――――――――――+―――――――――――――――|→
   0                               5                              10

3. How much do you love your partner?

   ←|―――――――――――――――+―――――――――――――――|→
   0                               5                              10

4. Does being in love mean putting your partner before yourself? Why or why not?

   _____

   _____

5. How did it feel falling/being in love?

   _____

   _____

6. How often do you say "I love you" to one another? _____

6A. How important is it that your partner says "I love you" to you? _____

6B. The singer, Extreme, in his song *More Than Words,* tells his partner not to say "I love you," but to show it. Do you agree? Explain.

_____

_____

7. List the ways you and your partner show love to each other.

_____   _____   _____   _____

_____   _____   _____   _____

8. What is your relationship status?
☐ In a Relationship
☐ Engaged
☐ Married

9. Fill in this timeline for you and your partner:

First Date: _____

Became Official: _____

Proposal: _____

Married: _____

Today's Date: _____

10. How would you rate your relationship?

◀━━━━━━━━━━━━━━━┼━━━━━━━━━━━━━━━▶

0                                5                                10

11. Have you leaned on your love for one another during difficult times? If so, explain.

_____

_____

_____

_____

12. Explain the ways in which both of you can strengthen the love you have for one another.

_____

_____

_____

_____

_____

_____

Name: _____     Hector Suco     Date: _____

# Love

This worksheet is for anyone currently in a romantic relationship.

1. What do you think love is? (Select all that apply)
   ☐ Feeling
   ☐ State of Mind
   ☐ Attitude
   ☐ Decision
   ☐ Other: _____

2. How much do you love yourself?

   ←|―――――――――――――|―――――――――――――|→
   0                             5                             10

3. How much do you love your partner?

   ←|―――――――――――――|―――――――――――――|→
   0                             5                             10

4. Does being in love mean putting your partner before yourself? Why or why not?

   _____

   _____

5. How did it feel falling/being in love?

   _____

   _____

6. How often do you say "I love you" to one another? _____

6A. How important is it that your partner says "I love you" to you? _____

6B. The singer, Extreme, in his song *More Than Words,* tells his partner not to say "I love you," but to show it. Do you agree? Explain.

_____

_____

7. List the ways you and your partner show love to each other.

_____   _____   _____   _____

_____   _____   _____   _____

8. What is your relationship status?
- ☐ In a Relationship
- ☐ Engaged
- ☐ Married

9. Fill in this timeline for you and your partner:

First Date: _____

Became Official: _____

Proposal: _____

Married: _____

Today's Date: _____

10. How would you rate your relationship?

◄――――――――――――――+――――――――――――――►
0                                        5                                        10

11. Have you leaned on your love for one another during difficult times? If so, explain.

_____

_____

_____

_____

12. Explain the ways in which both of you can strengthen the love you have for one another.

_____

_____

_____

_____

_____

Name: _____    Hector Suco    Date: _____

# Love

This worksheet is for anyone currently in a romantic relationship.

1. What do you think love is? (Select all that apply)
   ☐ Feeling
   ☐ State of Mind
   ☐ Attitude
   ☐ Decision
   ☐ Other: _____

2. How much do you love yourself?

   ⬅|—————————————————+—————————————————|➡
   0                  5                  10

3. How much do you love your partner?

   ⬅|—————————————————+—————————————————|➡
   0                  5                  10

4. Does being in love mean putting your partner before yourself? Why or why not?

   _____

   _____

5. How did it feel falling/being in love?

   _____

   _____

6. How often do you say "I love you" to one another? _____

6A. How important is it that your partner says "I love you" to you? _____

6B. The singer, Extreme, in his song *More Than Words,* tells his partner not to say "I love you," but to show it. Do you agree? Explain.

_____

_____

7. List the ways you and your partner show love to each other.

_____  _____  _____  _____

_____  _____  _____  _____

8. What is your relationship status?
- ☐ In a Relationship
- ☐ Engaged
- ☐ Married

9. Fill in this timeline for you and your partner:

First Date: _____

Became Official: _____

Proposal: _____

Married: _____

Today's Date: _____

10. How would you rate your relationship?

◄―――――――――――――――――|―――――――――――――――――►

0                                        5                                        10

11. Have you leaned on your love for one another during difficult times? If so, explain.

___

12. Explain the ways in which both of you can strengthen the love you have for one another.

___

Name: _____     Hector Suco     Date: _____

# Love

This worksheet is for anyone currently in a romantic relationship.

1. What do you think love is? (Select all that apply)
   - ☐ Feeling
   - ☐ State of Mind
   - ☐ Attitude
   - ☐ Decision
   - ☐ Other: _____

2. How much do you love yourself?

   0 —————————— 5 —————————— 10

3. How much do you love your partner?

   0 —————————— 5 —————————— 10

4. Does being in love mean putting your partner before yourself? Why or why not?

   _____

   _____

5. How did it feel falling/being in love?

   _____

   _____

6. How often do you say "I love you" to one another? _____

6A. How important is it that your partner says "I love you" to you? _____

6B. The singer, Extreme, in his song *More Than Words,* tells his partner not to say "I love you," but to show it. Do you agree? Explain.

_____

_____

7. List the ways you and your partner show love to each other.

_____   _____   _____   _____

_____   _____   _____   _____

8. What is your relationship status?
- ☐ In a Relationship
- ☐ Engaged
- ☐ Married

9. Fill in this timeline for you and your partner:

First Date: _____

Became Official: _____

Proposal: _____

Married: _____

Today's Date: _____

10. How would you rate your relationship?

⇔―――――――――――――|―――――――――――――⇔

0                                    5                                   10

11. Have you leaned on your love for one another during difficult times? If so, explain.

_____

_____

_____

_____

12. Explain the ways in which both of you can strengthen the love you have for one another.

_____

_____

_____

_____

_____

_____

Name: _____  Hector Suco  Date: _____

# Love

This worksheet is for anyone currently in a romantic relationship.

1. What do you think love is? (Select all that apply)
   - ☐ Feeling
   - ☐ State of Mind
   - ☐ Attitude
   - ☐ Decision
   - ☐ Other: _____

2. How much do you love yourself?

   0 —————————————— 5 —————————————— 10

3. How much do you love your partner?

   0 —————————————— 5 —————————————— 10

4. Does being in love mean putting your partner before yourself? Why or why not?

   _____

   _____

5. How did it feel falling/being in love?

   _____

   _____

6. How often do you say "I love you" to one another? _____

6A. How important is it that your partner says "I love you" to you? _____

6B. The singer, Extreme, in his song *More Than Words,* tells his partner not to say "I love you," but to show it. Do you agree? Explain.

_____

_____

7. List the ways you and your partner show love to each other.

_____  _____  _____  _____

_____  _____  _____  _____

8. What is your relationship status?
 ☐ In a Relationship
 ☐ Engaged
 ☐ Married

9. Fill in this timeline for you and your partner:

First Date: _____

Became Official: _____

Proposal: _____

Married: _____

Today's Date: _____

10. How would you rate your relationship?

0                5                10

11. Have you leaned on your love for one another during difficult times? If so, explain.

_____

_____

_____

_____

12. Explain the ways in which both of you can strengthen the love you have for one another.

_____

_____

_____

_____

_____

_____

# Love Worksheet Guide

1. Love is a term used to describe an array of feelings, states of mind, attitudes, etc. Some also say it is a conscious or subconscious decision one makes on a daily basis. Love can also be actions you take.

2. This is not about selfishness or self-righteousness; this is about the love you have for your identity and existence. For if you do not love yourself first, who can and who will?

3. I believe that, while love (and the answer to this question) is fluid, you either love someone or you do not. That love can increase or decrease over time and depending on different occurrences. However, do not confuse "loving" someone for "liking" them. Liking someone is easy and can change in an instant. For example, when our parents do something that frustrates us - we still love them, but we do not like them at that point in time because they are a source of stress.

4. Different people will have different answers to this question due to what they have been taught to believe, what they have seen within their own family, etc. There is no right or wrong answer. Some people strongly believe you must put your partner before yourself and sacrifice your happiness if it means they will be happy. Others think that they should love themselves first before loving others. Think hard on this one.

5. You should "feel" this answer. Remember what was happening or what it was like in that moment when you just *knew* you were in love with your partner.

6. The signer, Extreme, makes sense. It is very important that you understand the implications of saying, "I love you," before actually saying it. It means many things to different people.

Examples of showing love:

| Hold hands | Take them on a date | Set up candlelight dinner | Love note(s) | Leave a note in their lunch |
|---|---|---|---|---|
| Handmade gift | Flowers | Breakfast in bed | Use Google for more ideas | |

7. These can be anything from planning elaborate dates or surprises to taking out the trash every night or doing your partner's most hated chore for them so they do not have to. Love is not always in the big things - little gestures can be love too.

10. A relationship of any kind will always need work. If your answer and your partner's answer are different, talk to them about why they rated the relationship the way they did, explain why you rated it the way you did, and discuss how you can work together to improve it.

11. When people say, "have faith that everything will work out," they are also saying to use the love you have for one another to get you through tough times. But how will you do that exactly? Everyone's answers will differ. Find what works for the both of you.

12. Marriage Counselors: Marriage counselors are trained professionals who make it their mission to help you and your partner cultivate strong roots to ensure the healthy growth of your relationship. However, there are some that will say that couples/marriage counselors are a waste of money and time. There are those who go see a couple's counselor and their relationship flourishes.

Retreats: There are annual couple's retreats through religious affiliations or other organizations whose goal is to help strengthen the bonds of love.

Strengthening the bond you have with your partner is something you can work on every day in small ways, or less frequently in enormous ways. Which are you willing to try to strengthen the love you have for each other? What are you doing now that is working for the both of you? What have you already tried that has not worked?

I hope this has helped you.
Good luck on your journey.

Name: _____    Hector Suco    Date: _____

# Romance

1. How romantic are you?

2. How romantic is your partner?

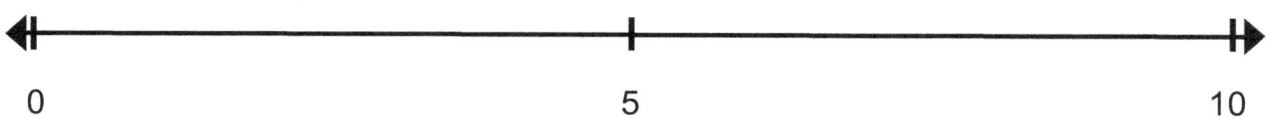

3. What is your definition of romance or being romantic?

_____

_____

_____

4. How important is romance to you in your relationship compared to other factors like communication, trust, intimacy, and respect?

_____

_____

_____

5. List ways that you would like your partner to be more romantic.

_____   _____   _____   _____

_____   _____   _____   _____

6. Ask your partner how they would like you to be more romantic to them.

_____   _____   _____   _____

_____   _____   _____   _____

Name: _____    Hector Suco    Date: _____

# Romance

1. How romantic are you?

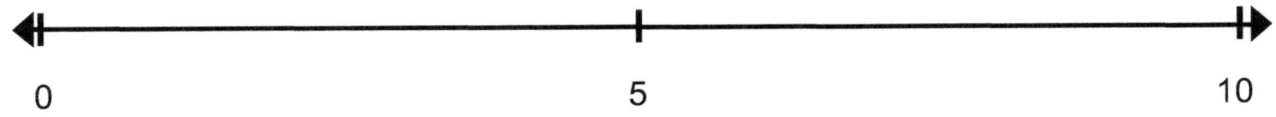

2. How romantic is your partner?

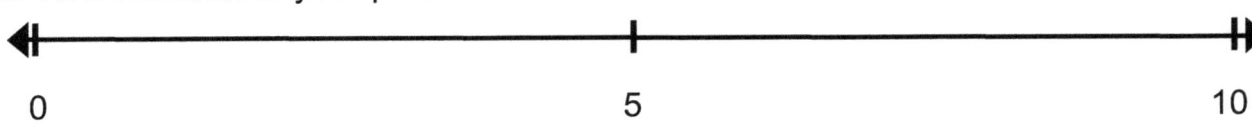

3. What is your definition of romance or being romantic?

_____
_____
_____

4. How important is romance to you in your relationship compared to other factors like communication, trust, intimacy, and respect?

_____
_____
_____

5. List ways that you would like your partner to be more romantic.

_____  _____  _____  _____  _____
_____  _____  _____  _____  _____

6. Ask your partner how they would like you to be more romantic to them.

_____  _____  _____  _____  _____
_____  _____  _____  _____  _____

Name: _____     Hector Suco     Date: _____

# Romance

1. How romantic are you?

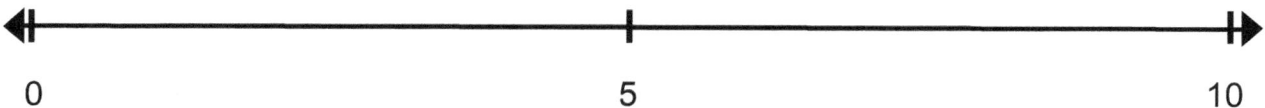

0                          5                          10

2. How romantic is your partner?

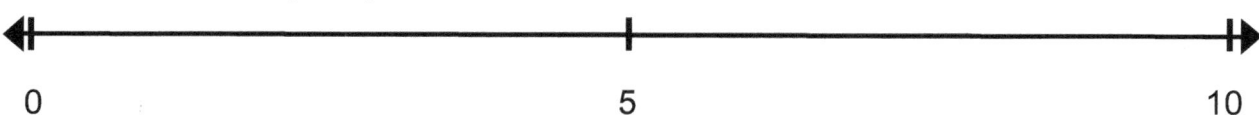

0                          5                          10

3. What is your definition of romance or being romantic?

_____

_____

_____

4. How important is romance to you in your relationship compared to other factors like communication, trust, intimacy, and respect?

_____

_____

_____

_____

5. List ways that you would like your partner to be more romantic.

_____  _____  _____  _____

_____  _____  _____  _____

6. Ask your partner how they would like you to be more romantic to them.

_____  _____  _____  _____

_____  _____  _____  _____

# Romance Worksheet Guide

1. & 2. Romance is not just about a husband bringing his wife flowers. Just like love, communication, and care, romance needs to be reciprocated. So, wives and/or the receivers in relationships need to reciprocate their love through romance in their own unique way. The answer lies in the communication you have with your partner. Hopefully, this worksheet will ignite that conversation.

3. Just like love, there is a dictionary meaning to romance. However, people will define it in different ways based on their views and values. According to Dictionary.com, romance is "to court or woo; treat with ardor or chivalry."

4. Where would you place romance in the order of the values that make a good relationship strong? Romance tends to be the spice of any relationship, however, it is not the full meal. People can say, "the romance is dead." But that does not mean the relationship is. Maybe, all that the relationship needs is, to quote Emeril Lagasse, "to bring it up a notch."

5. & 6. Here are examples from an exhaustive list of ways to be romantic.

| Classic | Creative | Adventurous | Extra |
| --- | --- | --- | --- |
| Flowers | Scavenger hunt | Hiking | Sunrise |
| Chocolate | Escape room | Water sports | Sunset |
| Love Letter | Create gift | Walk on the beach | Getaway |
| Romantic Movie | Create something | Snow Sports | Watch the stars |
| Gifts | Rose petals leading somewhere | Dance in the rain | Romantic Destinations |
| Candlelight Dinner | Blindfold to somewhere | Extreme sports | Relationship to the next level |

Name: _____    Hector Suco    Date: _____

# A Relationship Letter Of Gratitude

**The Gratitude Letter**

1. Write your partner a letter expressing why you are grateful for having them in your life. Be concrete and specific. How have they influenced your life? What have they taught you? How is your life better because of them? Take two weeks drafting your letter. You may use the next page as draft space. You should use a word processing program like Microsoft Word or Google Docs to write your letter. Once you have your letter finished, read it out loud to your partner and talk about the content.

2. After writing your letter and reading your letter to them, write about your reactions below. How did this experience make you feel?

_____

_____

_____

_____

_____

_____

# A Letter Of Gratitude

Dear _____,

_____
_____
_____
_____
_____
_____
_____
_____
_____
_____

With Love,

_____

Name: _____  Hector Suco  Date: _____

# A Relationship Letter Of Gratitude

## The Gratitude Letter

1. Write your partner a letter expressing why you are grateful for having them in your life. Be concrete and specific. How have they influenced your life? What have they taught you? How is your life better because of them? Take two weeks drafting your letter. You may use the next page as draft space. You should use a word processing program like Microsoft Word or Google Docs to write your letter. Once you have your letter finished, read it out loud to your partner and talk about the content.

2. After writing your letter and reading your letter to them, write about your reactions below. How did this experience make you feel?

_____
_____
_____
_____
_____
_____

# A Letter Of Gratitude

Dear _____,

_____
_____
_____
_____
_____
_____
_____
_____
_____
_____
_____

With Love,


_____

Name: _____  Hector Suco  Date: _____

# A Relationship Letter Of Gratitude

**The Gratitude Letter**

1. Write your partner a letter expressing why you are grateful for having them in your life. Be concrete and specific. How have they influenced your life? What have they taught you? How is your life better because of them? Take two weeks drafting your letter. You may use the next page as draft space. You should use a word processing program like Microsoft Word or Google Docs to write your letter. Once you have your letter finished, read it out loud to your partner and talk about the content.

2. After writing your letter and reading your letter to them, write about your reactions below. How did this experience make you feel?

_____

_____

_____

_____

_____

_____

# A Letter Of Gratitude

Dear _____,

_____
_____
_____
_____
_____
_____
_____
_____
_____
_____

With Love,

_____

Name: _____     Hector Suco     Date: _____

# A Relationship Letter Of Gratitude

**The Gratitude Letter**

1. Write your partner a letter expressing why you are grateful for having them in your life. Be concrete and specific. How have they influenced your life? What have they taught you? How is your life better because of them? Take two weeks drafting your letter. You may use the next page as draft space. You should use a word processing program like Microsoft Word or Google Docs to write your letter. Once you have your letter finished, read it out loud to your partner and talk about the content.

2. After writing your letter and reading your letter to them, write about your reactions below. How did this experience make you feel?

_____

_____

_____

_____

_____

_____

# A Letter Of Gratitude

Dear _____,

_____
_____
_____
_____
_____
_____
_____
_____
_____
_____
_____

With Love,

_____

Name: _____  Hector Suco  Date: _____

# A Relationship Letter Of Gratitude

**The Gratitude Letter**

1. Write your partner a letter expressing why you are grateful for having them in your life. Be concrete and specific. How have they influenced your life? What have they taught you? How is your life better because of them? Take two weeks drafting your letter. You may use the next page as draft space. You should use a word processing program like Microsoft Word or Google Docs to write your letter. Once you have your letter finished, read it out loud to your partner and talk about the content.

2. After writing your letter and reading your letter to them, write about your reactions below. How did this experience make you feel?

_____

_____

_____

_____

_____

_____

# A Letter Of Gratitude

Dear _____,

_____

_____

_____

_____

_____

_____

_____

_____

_____

_____

_____

With Love,

_____

Name: _____   Hector Suco   Date: _____

# Jealousy

1. Are you currently in a relationship, dating someone, or interested in someone?
☐ Yes
☐ No (Skip to #6)

2. Are you jealous of losing your partner (or the person you're interested in) to someone else?
☐ Yes
☐ No (Skip to #6)

3. What is the basis for your feelings of jealousy?

_____

_____

_____

4. Do you think that the jealousy is stemming from your frustrations towards your partner? What are those frustrations?

_____

_____

_____

5. Would you be willing to let your partner go out with their friends, but without you?

_____

_____

6. In general, do you consider yourself a jealous person?

_____

_____

Name: _____  Hector Suco    Date: _____

# Jealousy

1. Are you currently in a relationship, dating someone, or interested in someone?
   ☐ Yes
   ☐ No (Skip to #6)

2. Are you jealous of losing your partner (or the person you're interested in) to someone else?
   ☐ Yes
   ☐ No (Skip to #6)

3. What is the basis for your feelings of jealousy?

   _____

   _____

   _____

4. Do you think that the jealousy is stemming from your frustrations towards your partner? What are those frustrations?

   _____

   _____

   _____

5. Would you be willing to let your partner go out with their friends, but without you?

   _____

   _____

6. In general, do you consider yourself a jealous person?

   _____

   _____

Name: _____  Hector Suco    Date: _____

# Jealousy

1. Are you currently in a relationship, dating someone, or interested in someone?
   ☐ Yes
   ☐ No (Skip to #6)

2. Are you jealous of losing your partner (or the person you're interested in) to someone else?
   ☐ Yes
   ☐ No (Skip to #6)

3. What is the basis for your feelings of jealousy?

   _____

   _____

   _____

4. Do you think that the jealousy is stemming from your frustrations towards your partner? What are those frustrations?

   _____

   _____

   _____

5. Would you be willing to let your partner go out with their friends, but without you?

   _____

   _____

6. In general, do you consider yourself a jealous person?

   _____

   _____

# Jealousy Worksheet Guide

Jealousy is the fear of losing a partner to someone else. Envy is the want to have what others have. Jealousy usually applies to people who are in relationships, dating, or have their eye on someone.

2. If you picked yes, do you know who this other person is? What evidence do you have that they are trying to take your partner away from you? Have you confronted your partner about this person? Are you afraid of losing them in general? Why?

3. If your partner has betrayed your trust before, what other reasons do you have for being jealous?

4. Frustrations that build up can cause anger, which can cause unfounded jealousy. Whatever your issues are, discuss them with your partner.

5. Your partner not allowing you to go out without them signals a trust issue. Conversely, you not allowing your partner to go out without you means that you do not trust them. Think about why that is. Do you have a belief that you should always be with your partner around others, or have they done anything that has bothered you in the past? Discuss this with them because letting your partner go out without you shows that you trust them, and you should be able to trust them if you want your relationship to last.

6. Look back at your life and your other relationships to compare if you have been a jealous person throughout. If these feelings are new, why are you having them? Pay attention to your relationships with friends, family, and partners. What has caused your jealousy in the past?

I hope this has helped you.
Good luck on your journey.

Name: _____     Hector Suco     Date: _____

# Relationship Trust

This worksheet is to be filled out by someone currently in a relationship. If a trust has been broken, please use the Romantic Betrayed or Romantic Betrayer Worksheet.

1. List some or all of the spoken and unspoken agreements you have with your partner and your relationship.

| Spoken Agreements or Courtesies (No cheating, Dinner at the table, etc.) | Unspoken Agreements or Courtesies (Saying "good morning" everyday, No flirting, etc.) |
|---|---|
|  |  |
|  |  |
|  |  |
|  |  |
|  |  |
|  |  |
|  |  |

2. How important is honesty in your relationship?

_____

_____

3. How often do you say, "I'm sorry" and/or admit to your mistakes?

_____
_____

4. Do you two share a bank account? Would you trust your partner if they wanted their own bank account? Why or why not?

_____
_____

5. What does the phrase "trust takes years to build, seconds to break, and forever to repair" mean to you?

_____
_____

6. What are some ways you can build trust with your partner?

_____
_____

7. What are some ways your partner can build trust with you?

_____
_____

Name: _____    Hector Suco    Date: _____

# Relationship Trust

This worksheet is to be filled out by someone currently in a relationship. If a trust has been broken, please use the Romantic Betrayed or Romantic Betrayer Worksheet.

1. List some or all of the spoken and unspoken agreements you have with your partner and your relationship.

| Spoken Agreements or Courtesies (No cheating, Dinner at the table, etc.) | Unspoken Agreements or Courtesies (Saying "good morning" everyday, No flirting, etc.) |
|---|---|
|  |  |
|  |  |
|  |  |
|  |  |
|  |  |
|  |  |
|  |  |

2. How important is honesty in your relationship?

_____

_____

3. How often do you say, "I'm sorry" and/or admit to your mistakes?

_____

_____

4. Do you two share a bank account? Would you trust your partner if they wanted their own bank account? Why or why not?

_____

_____

5. What does the phrase "trust takes years to build, seconds to break, and forever to repair" mean to you?

_____

_____

6. What are some ways you can build trust with your partner?

_____

_____

7. What are some ways your partner can build trust with you?

_____

_____

# Relationship Trust Worksheet Guide

1. Examples of spoken and/or unspoken agreements would be not cheating, always know each others whereabouts, active listening, no lying, no gambling, how to handle financial issues, how to deal with the in-laws, parenting styles (how to discipline, extracurricular activities, when to expose them to x, y, & z), always mention when one changes their mind on important issues, not going to sleep angry, not arguing in front of children, or any other "rules" you just know you need to respect.

2. Honesty is the best policy. It is one of the anchors of a healthy relationship and it holds them together like the brick and mortar in a wall.

3. Pride is a poison that will rot any relationship to its core. One of you has to come out and say it, "I was wrong, you were right." Now, it goes both ways. Your partner needs to be open to admitting the mistakes they make as well. That is why communication is key. Remember that a relationship is two people becoming one, not two people fighting until one is left standing - that's *Survivor*.

4. Having a joint account, separate accounts, or both is a decision that all couples need to make together. If a couple is on the fence about which to have, write the pros and cons of each and come to an agreement. Some people prefer the idea of financial independence as opposed to a "what's yours is mine and what's mine is yours" mentality. Decide together and, no matter what happens, do not keep secrets.

5. The phrase "trust takes years to build, seconds to break, and forever to repair" has a deep meaning. As one of the foundations of any functional relationship (self, romantic, familial, friendship), trust is like the roots of a tree. Communication makes up the roots that feed the tree and the main structure, the trunk, is honesty. A weak trunk (lack of honesty) causes the leaves (trust) to die, and a lack of communication (bad roots) starves the whole tree. This causes the tree to fall. That's why, like a tree, relationships "take years to build, seconds to break, and forever to repair."

6. & 7. There are many ways you can build and earn the trust of others. Examples include:

| Reliability | Honesty | Open | Ethical | Morality |
|---|---|---|---|---|
| Keeping your word | Telling the truth | Saying more than is needed | Having strong morals | Being loyal |
| Not canceling plans | Owning up to your mistakes | Showing others you care | Showing fairness | Show more awareness |
| Keeping promises | Be tactful and constructive | Do not omit important things | Staying neutral during difficult times | Stay away from double standards |

I hope this has helped you.
Good luck on your journey.

Name: _____  Hector Suco  Date: _____

# Break-Up

This worksheet is for anyone who was/is in a relationship or engaged. If you were/are married, use the Marriage Separation Worksheet or Divorce Worksheet.

1. How would you describe your current situation?

|  | Status | Definition | Go To: |
|---|---|---|---|
| ☐ | Not Talking, But Still Together | Still together, no form of communication. | Question #2 only, then use my Relationship Conflict Resolution Worksheet |
| ☐ | On A Break | Still talking. Not exclusive; Can date/see other people. | Question #2; Stop at #6 |
| ☐ | Broke Up, Still Talking | Still talking as friends, hanging out. | Question #7; Stop at #12 |
| ☐ | Broke Up, Not Talking | No form of communication. | Question #10 |
| ☐ | Friends With Benefits | Sexual relationship with no feelings. | Use my Friends With Benefits Worksheet |

2. What is/are the issue(s) in the relationship? How can it be fixed? What will it take to make the relationship work again?

_____

_____

3. Who initiated the break or break-up?
   ☐ Myself
   ☐ My Partner
   ☐ It was mutual

4. Have you or your partner gone on dates with other people? Have you told each other?

_____

5. If you have decided to "take a break", what are the mutual boundaries you and your partner have set for this break?

_____   _____

_____   _____

6. Is there a time limit to this break? If so, how long is it? If not, what would you want it to be?

_____

7. When you hang out with your ex, is it just the two of you or are you with other people?

_____

8. Is there a chance your relationship can be saved? Explain.

_____

_____

9. Have you ever called your ex just to have sex; had sex with your partner while on a break; had a "friends with benefits" relationship with your ex?

_____

10. Who broke up with whom?
- ☐ I broke up with them (Go to #11)
- ☐ They broke up with me (Go to #11A)
- ☐ Mutual (Go to #11)

11. Do you regret your decision?   ☐ Yes (Go to 11A)   ☐ No (Go to #14)

11A. Would you want to try and get back together?
- ☐ Yes (Go to #12; Skip #13)
- ☐ Yes, but they are seeing someone else (Go to #12; Skip #13)
- ☐ I do not know (Go to #13)
- ☐ No (Go to #14)

12. Have you told them how you feel?

☐ Yes: What did they say? _____

☐ No: Why not? _____

\*\*\*The rest of this worksheet is about the actual break up. Feel free to stop here or continue.\*\*\*

| 13. Below, list their positive and negative attributes to compare. Then, describe how you think life will be like in the future with and without this person in your life. ||
|---|---|
| Positive Attributes: | Negative Attributes: |
|  |  |
|  |  |
|  |  |
|  |  |
| Describe what life will be like in the future… ||
| …with them. | …without them. |
|  |  |
|  |  |
|  |  |
|  |  |

14. How do you feel about the break up?
- ☐ Ecstatic (Go to #20)
- ☐ Happy (Go to #20)
- ☐ I do not know (Go to #15)
- ☐ Sad (Go to #15)
- ☐ Depressed (Go to #15)

15. Where are you in the 5 Stages of Grief?

☐ Denial  ☐ Anger  ☐ Bargaining  ☐ Depression  ☐ Acceptance

16. How much time have you spent thinking about this break up?

_____

17. Write down some of the thoughts you have had about the break up.

_____

_____

_____

18. Do you believe in a higher power that is helping and guiding you?

_____

19. Do you believe there's a divine plan that is set for you?

_____

20. What did you learn from this experience?

_____

_____

_____

21. Were there mistakes made? Explain.

_____

_____

_____

22. How will things be different next time?

_____

_____

_____

Name: _____    Hector Suco    Date: _____

# Break-Up

This worksheet is for anyone who was/is in a relationship or engaged. If you were/are married, use the Marriage Separation Worksheet or Divorce Worksheet.

1. How would you describe your current situation?

|   | **Status** | **Definition** | **Go To:** |
|---|---|---|---|
| ☐ | Not Talking, But Still Together | Still together, no form of communication. | Question #2 only, then use my Relationship Conflict Resolution Worksheet |
| ☐ | On A Break | Still talking. Not exclusive; Can date/see other people. | Question #2; Stop at #6 |
| ☐ | Broke Up, Still Talking | Still talking as friends, hanging out. | Question #7; Stop at #12 |
| ☐ | Broke Up, Not Talking | No form of communication. | Question #10 |
| ☐ | Friends With Benefits | Sexual relationship with no feelings. | Use my Friends With Benefits Worksheet |

2. What is/are the issue(s) in the relationship? How can it be fixed? What will it take to make the relationship work again?

_____

_____

3. Who initiated the break or break-up?
  ☐ Myself
  ☐ My Partner
  ☐ It was mutual

4. Have you or your partner gone on dates with other people? Have you told each other?

_____

5. If you have decided to "take a break", what are the mutual boundaries you and your partner have set for this break?

_____   _____

_____   _____

6. Is there a time limit to this break? If so, how long is it? If not, what would you want it to be?

_____

7. When you hang out with your ex, is it just the two of you or are you with other people?

_____

8. Is there a chance your relationship can be saved? Explain.

_____

_____

9. Have you ever called your ex just to have sex; had sex with your partner while on a break; had a "friends with benefits" relationship with your ex?

_____

10. Who broke up with whom?
- ☐ I broke up with them (Go to #11)
- ☐ They broke up with me (Go to #11A)
- ☐ Mutual (Go to #11)

11. Do you regret your decision?   ☐ Yes (Go to 11A)   ☐ No (Go to #14)

11A. Would you want to try and get back together?
- ☐ Yes (Go to #12; Skip #13)
- ☐ Yes, but they are seeing someone else (Go to #12; Skip #13)
- ☐ I do not know (Go to #13)
- ☐ No (Go to #14)

12. Have you told them how you feel?

☐ Yes: What did they say? _____

☐ No: Why not? _____

***The rest of this worksheet is about the actual break up. Feel free to stop here or continue.***

| 13. Below, list their positive and negative attributes to compare. Then, describe how you think life will be like in the future with and without this person in your life. ||
|---|---|
| Positive Attributes: | Negative Attributes: |
|  |  |
|  |  |
|  |  |
|  |  |
| Describe what life will be like in the future… ||
| …with them. | …without them. |
|  |  |
|  |  |
|  |  |
|  |  |

14. How do you feel about the break up?
- ☐ Ecstatic (Go to #20)
- ☐ Happy (Go to #20)
- ☐ I do not know (Go to #15)
- ☐ Sad (Go to #15)
- ☐ Depressed (Go to #15)

15. Where are you in the 5 Stages of Grief?

☐ Denial ☐ Anger ☐ Bargaining ☐ Depression ☐ Acceptance

16. How much time have you spent thinking about this break up?

_____

17. Write down some of the thoughts you have had about the break up.

_____

_____

_____

18. Do you believe in a higher power that is helping and guiding you?

_____

19. Do you believe there's a divine plan that is set for you?

_____

20. What did you learn from this experience?

_____

_____

_____

21. Were there mistakes made? Explain.

_____

_____

_____

22. How will things be different next time?

_____

_____

_____

# Break Up Worksheet Guide

1. Everyone has different ideas of what breaking up means, and not every break up is the same. These particular descriptions are meant to broadly cover everything in the dating spectrum. These definitions are meant to guide the reader to their next question.

2. Disagreements will always happen in relationships. Some will last minutes, while others can last for weeks. The causes vary (and are too numerous to list), but talking with your partner can solve almost all of them. An angry outburst can also cause disagreements. How can it be fixed? Can you compromise? Decide what needs to be done so everyone feels like they have been heard. Then, find an agreeable solution together.

3. - 6. If you've ever seen the TV show, *Friends*, then you know all about Rachel and Ross and their relationship rollercoaster. Rachel wanted "a break" from her relationship with Ross. The expectations of the break were never discussed. Ross thought that she meant that she wanted to end the relationship, while Rachel meant that she wanted them to spend some time apart without ending their relationship. Ross sleeps with another woman and gets caught by Rachel. Rachel sees this as a betrayal, while Ross justifies it by saying "we were on a break." That concept continues to come up throughout the series, but also demonstrates the potential problems when two people "take a break" from each other. If you want to or are on a break right now, set boundaries, set a time limit, and be honest with each other about what you want/expect each other to do or not do during the break.

7. - 8. I admire two people that can end a relationship and are still able to be friends. It not only shows civility, but also shows admiration and value for each other. At the same time, keeping a friendship can be difficult to do without hoping for the future. If you find yourself on a date-like outing with your ex, self-reflect on what you want from them. Do you want to get back together? Also, try to find out their views. Do they want to get back together with you? If there are children involved, it is a good idea to stay friends with your ex for the child(ren).

9. According to the most accepted definition on Urban Dictionary, a booty call is "A late night summons -- often made via telephone -- to arrange clandestine sexual liaisons on an ad hoc basis." One or more booty calls with your ex can turn into trying to rekindle your relationship or establish a friends with benefits relationship. Multiple occurrences should bring up questions about where this relationship is going. Feelings can get involved if this continues. As always, be diligent and use protection to prevent STD's, STI's, and unwanted pregnancies.

11A. If they are seeing someone else, be cautious and respectful of their current relationship. "I want them to be with me and no one else" is selfish, unfair, and mean. They do not depend on you for their happiness and you should not depend on them for yours.

12. If they say "yes", this paves the way for a reunion. A "maybe" or "I need time to think about it" means that you should give them space and time and make sure that you remain respectful. A no is unfortunate. You need to decide whether or not you want to stay friends with them. If you cannot, then try to move on and start letting go.

13. If you do not know if you want to try things again with your ex, write down their positive and negative attributes as well as what a potential future with them looks like, then compare. This can make it easier for you to decide. You can also show them this worksheet to try and start a dialogue with your ex.

14. Be honest about your feelings. You can use what you wrote for #13 to help you.

15. The 5 Stages of Grief are listed below:

| 1. Denial | "We're not really broken up." "They're just kidding." "They're just trying to scare me." "We're still together." "They're going to want me back." |
|---|---|
| 2. Anger | "What did I do wrong?" "How could I be so stupid?" "It is their fault." |
| 3. Bargaining | "What if I change?" "What can I do to get them back?" "I can do better if they just give me a chance." |
| 4. Depression | "I suck at being a partner." "It was never meant to be." "I'll never find true love." "Why is this happening to me?" |
| 5. Acceptance | "I will be okay." "I will find true love again." "It is better this way." "I've learned a lot from this experience." |

16. Time is very valuable thing. Once it passes, you can never get it back. The more time you spend thinking about this break up, the less time you will have to enjoy yourself and focus on the things you do have that make you happy.

17. Self-talk, termed by Albert Ellis, refers to the running commentary that goes on in your mind during the day. Most of it means very little, but it can become a problem when your thinking turns into harmful beliefs about yourself and/or your ex. Many studies have found a link between irrational beliefs and anxiety. Look for reasons (even little ones) to be satisfied and happy with your life, no matter what you are going through. Always try to find the silver lining.

"Psychologist Ethan Kross found that how people conduct their inner monologues has an enormous effect on their success in life. Talk to yourself with the pronoun *I*, for instance, and you're likely to fluster and perform poorly in stressful circumstances. Address yourself by your name and your chances of acing a host of tasks, from speech making to self-advocacy, suddenly soar."
-Pamela Weintraub "The Voice of Reason"
*Psychology Today*
May 4th, 2015

18. - 19. Reflect on how you feel about divine intervention, a higher power, and religion as it relates to fate, etc.

20. How have you grown or changed in the time you spent in the relationship?

21. – 22. How are you going to make sure those mistakes do not happen again in any future relationship of yours?

I hope this has helped you.
Good luck on your journey.

Name: _____     Hector Suco     Date: _____

# Is Marriage For You?

This worksheet is to be filled out by someone who is single or is thinking about getting married. This worksheet is similar to my Engagement Worksheet.

1. What is your relationship status?
   - ☐ Single (Answer #5, 6, 8, & 9 only)
   - ☐ Official Couple
   - ☐ Engaged
   - ☐ Married

2. How long have you been in this relationship? _____

3. How would you rate your relationship?

   ◄|―――――――――――――――|―――――――――――――――|► 
   0                               5                              10

4. Why did you rate your relationship that way?

   _____

   _____

5. Do you want to get married?

   ☐ Yes: Why?

   _____

   _____

   ☐ No: Why not?

   _____

   _____

   ☐ I do not know. Explain:

   _____

6. How sure are you that you want to get married?

```
0%                          50%                        100%
```

7. Would you sacrifice your life for your partner?

☐ Yes
☐ No
☐ I do not know

Explain your answer:
_____
_____

8. Can you think of any reason(s) you shouldn't get married?
_____
_____
_____

9. What does marriage mean to you?
_____
_____
_____

# Communication

10. How long does it take for you and your partner to get over an argument?

_____

_____

11. Do you and/or your partner ever give each other the silent treatment? If so, how long does it last?

_____

_____

12. What role does pride play in your relationship?

_____

_____

13. How challenging is it for you or your partner to say, "I was wrong, you were right"?

_____

_____

# Finances

Estimate your answers.

14. How many credit cards do you have? _____

15. How many credit cards does your partner have? _____

16. How much debt do you have? _____

17. How much debt does your partner have? _____

18. Which one of you makes more money? _____

19. Does the answer to #18 bother you? _____

Name: _____  Hector Suco  Date: _____

# Is Marriage For You?

This worksheet is to be filled out by someone who is single or is thinking about getting married. This worksheet is similar to my Engagement Worksheet.

1. What is your relationship status?
- ☐ Single (Answer #5, 6, 8, & 9 only)
- ☐ Official Couple
- ☐ Engaged
- ☐ Married

2. How long have you been in this relationship? _____

3. How would you rate your relationship?

⇤————————————|————————————⇥
0                          5                          10

4. Why did you rate your relationship that way?

_____

_____

5. Do you want to get married?

☐ Yes: Why?

_____

_____

☐ No: Why not?

_____

_____

☐ I do not know. Explain:

_____

_____

6. How sure are you that you want to get married?

|←―――――――――――――――+―――――――――――――――→|
0%                              50%                              100%

7. Would you sacrifice your life for your partner?

☐ Yes
☐ No
☐ I do not know

Explain your answer:
_____
_____

8. Can you think of any reason(s) you shouldn't get married?
_____
_____
_____

9. What does marriage mean to you?
_____
_____
_____

## Communication

10. How long does it take for you and your partner to get over an argument?

_____

_____

11. Do you and/or your partner ever give each other the silent treatment? If so, how long does it last?

_____

_____

12. What role does pride play in your relationship?

_____

_____

13. How challenging is it for you or your partner to say, "I was wrong, you were right"?

_____

_____

## Finances

Estimate your answers.

14. How many credit cards do you have? _____

15. How many credit cards does your partner have? _____

16. How much debt do you have? _____

17. How much debt does your partner have? _____

18. Which one of you makes more money? _____

19. Does the answer to #18 bother you? _____

# Is Marriage For You? Worksheet Guide

1. This worksheet is ideal for someone who is already in a relationship. Single people may fill out this worksheet as a test to gauge whether marriage is for them or not on a general level.

2. The length of your relationship can influence how you feel about marriage. Thinking about it after too short of a time can be intimidating, while thinking about it after many years can make it seem unimportant or unnecessary.

3. & 4. If you think your rating is low, you should work on your relationship before considering marriage. Discuss why you rated it this way with your partner. Your partner's rating of the relationship equally matters.

5. Be honest with yourself. This is the most important question in the worksheet. If you answered no or I do not know, explain.

6. You need to be 100% sure that you are ready to make a lifelong commitment to this person through thick and thin. You cannot be 60% sure, you cannot be 80% sure, you cannot have any doubt in your mind. If you're only 99.9% sure, look for that last bit of confidence somewhere, it is there, you just need to find it.

7. The bottom line here is whether or not you value your partner's life over your own. Loving someone is often seen as putting someone else's needs and wants above your own. How do you feel about this?

8. Deal breakers are issues couples need to hash out or have an understanding of before moving forward in their relationship. What are some of your *musts* before you to enter into a marriage? Also, you may want to use my Relationship Deal Breakers Worksheet for a more in-depth look at deal breakers.

9. There's a dictionary definition to marriage. Every religion has their definition to marriage. You have to ask yourself, "What does the word marriage mean to me?"

10. – 13. "Never go to bed angry at each other." It is easier said than done. The longer it takes for you and your partner to talk out your problems, the harder things are likely to be. Sometimes, for the sake of your relationship, one of you has to come out and say it, "I was wrong, you were right." However, this goes both ways. You both need to admit to shortcomings. That is why communication is key. Remember that marriage is two people becoming one, not two people fighting and one is left standing. That's *Survivor*.

14. – 19. Jan D. Anderson, Ph.D, performed a study in 2000 that indicated statistically significant relationships between financial problems and divorce. You need to be in agreement on major issues when it comes to finances, including how much to spend and save. Usually, this can be solved with a budget. Discuss your finances with your partner. Two heads are better than one.
Source: https://digitalcommons.usu.edu/etd/2445

I hope this has helped you.
Good luck on your journey.

Name: _____    Hector Suco    Date: _____

# Engagement

This worksheet is for anyone who is engaged. This worksheet and my Is Marriage For You Worksheet are similar.

1. Which statement best describes your situation?
- ☐ I am planning to propose to my partner.
- ☐ I am thinking about proposing to my partner.
- ☐ I think that my partner will propose to me soon.
- ☐ I want my partner to propose to me.
- ☐ My partner and I are engaged. (Go to #1A)

1A. When is your wedding? _____

2. How long have you been in this relationship? _____

3. How would you rate your relationship?

```
+——————————————+——————————————+
0              5              10
```

4. Do you want to get married?

Yes: Why? _____

_____

No: Why not? _____

_____

I do not know. Explain:

_____

_____

5. How sure are you that you want to get married?

```
+——————————————+——————————————+
0%            50%            100%
```

178

6. What does marriage mean to you?

_____

_____

7. Would you sacrifice your life for your partner?
☐ Yes
☐ No
☐ I do not know

Explain your answer:

_____

_____

8. How are you going to support each other?

_____

_____

9. Have you discussed your deal breakers with each other?

_____

_____

10. Do your families approve of each other?

_____

_____

11. What kind of wedding do you want?

_____

_____

# Communication

12. How long does it take for you and your partner to get over an argument?
_____

13. Do you and/or your partner ever give the silent treatment? If so, how long does it last?
_____

14. What role does pride play in your relationship?
_____

15. How challenging is it for you or your partner to say, "I was wrong, you were right"?
_____
_____

# Finances

Estimate your answers.

16. How many credit cards do you have? _____

17. How many credit cards does your partner have? _____

18. How much debt do you have? _____

19. How much debt does your partner have? _____

20. Which one of you makes more money? _____

21. Does that bother you? Explain: _____

Name: _____  Hector Suco   Date: _____

# Engagement

This worksheet is for anyone who is engaged. This worksheet and my Is Marriage For You Worksheet are similar.

1. Which statement best describes your situation?
- ☐ I am planning to propose to my partner.
- ☐ I am thinking about proposing to my partner.
- ☐ I think that my partner will propose to me soon.
- ☐ I want my partner to propose to me.
- ☐ My partner and I are engaged. (Go to #1A)

1A. When is your wedding? _____

2. How long have you been in this relationship? _____

3. How would you rate your relationship?

```
<---+--------------------+--------------------+--->
    0                    5                    10
```

4. Do you want to get married?

Yes: Why? _____

_____

No: Why not? _____

_____

I do not know. Explain:

_____

_____

5. How sure are you that you want to get married?

```
<---+--------------------+--------------------+--->
   0%                   50%                  100%
```

6. What does marriage mean to you?

_____

_____

7. Would you sacrifice your life for your partner?
- ☐ Yes
- ☐ No
- ☐ I do not know

Explain your answer:

_____

_____

8. How are you going to support each other?

_____

_____

9. Have you discussed your deal breakers with each other?

_____

_____

10. Do your families approve of each other?

_____

_____

11. What kind of wedding do you want?

_____

_____

# Communication

12. How long does it take for you and your partner to get over an argument?
_____

13. Do you and/or your partner ever give the silent treatment? If so, how long does it last?
_____

14. What role does pride play in your relationship?
_____

15. How challenging is it for you or your partner to say, "I was wrong, you were right"?
_____
_____

# Finances

Estimate your answers.

16. How many credit cards do you have? _____

17. How many credit cards does your partner have? _____

18. How much debt do you have? _____

19. How much debt does your partner have? _____

20. Which one of you makes more money? _____

21. Does that bother you? Explain: _____

# Engagement Worksheet Guide

This worksheet is ideal for anyone who is about to get engaged or is already engaged. Though some people are confident about proposing, some may be questioning their life changing decision. This worksheet will work for both.

2. The length of your relationship can and should affect how you feel about marrying your partner. If you get married too quickly, you may not know enough about your partner - you may find some things that would make you reconsider marriage after it is too late. On the other hand, if you have spent a long time in your relationship, you may start to think nothing will really change just because you get married. Let your experience guide your decision, but do not let that be the only thing.

3. If your rating is from 1 – 3, then you need to work on your relationship before you start thinking about marriage. If your rating is between a 4 – 8, then your relationship needs more work. If your rating is a 9 or 10, then you might be ready for marriage. Your partner's rating is an equally important factor.

4. Be honest with yourself. This is the most important question of the worksheet.

5. You have to be 100% sure about this life-changing decision. If you're not 100% sure, think about what you need in order to get there. Talk about this with your partner.

6. There's a dictionary definition to marriage. Every religion has their definition to marriage as well. You have to ask yourself, "what does the word marriage mean to me?"

7. You hear it in love songs, you see it in the movies and it is a question that should be a yes. If you will not die for this person, what will you give up for the person that completes you? What sacrifices will you make in the relationship?

8. Ways to support each other is be empathetic, ask about their needs, support their ideas and hobbies, show affection, be understanding, be proud of them, etc.

9. Use my Relationship Deal Breakers Worksheet.

10. Personal stories from families and friends, as well as jokes, center on the "dreaded in-laws." Movies such as Monster-In-Law, My Big Fat Greek Wedding, Meet The Parents, and Guess Who's Coming to Dinner all showcase what obstacles can occur when families of engaged couples meet. All these movies have happy endings that surround the love of the couple as overcoming all the shortcomings their families exemplify. Tread lightly and know the line that you should not cross when dealing with your partner's parents. Each of you have been

raised in different homes, values, and rules, spoken and unspoken. If you have a problem, society states that you should tell your partner that will then handle it, though many would also say it depends on what kind of relationship you have with your in-laws. Like I said, tread lightly.

11. Whether you want to elope, have a small wedding, a destination wedding, a wedding at the beach, or an all out extravaganza, decide on what type of wedding will make both of you happy. Don't break your budget and do depend on others when you are feeling too stressed with the wedding.

12. – 15. "Never go to bed angry at each other." It is easier said than done. The longer it takes for you and your partner to talk out your problems, the harder things are likely to be. Sometimes, for the sake of your relationship, one of you has to come out and say it, "I was wrong, you were right." However, this goes both ways. You both need to admit to shortcomings. That is why communication is key. Remember that marriage is two people becoming one, not two people fighting and one is left standing. That's *Survivor*.

16. – 21. Jan D. Anderson, Ph.D., performed a study in 2000 that indicated statistically significant relationships between financial problems and divorce. You need to be in agreement on major issues when it comes to finances, including how much to spend and save. Usually, this can be solved with a budget. Discuss your finances with your partner. Two heads are better than one.

Source: https://digitalcommons.usu.edu/etd/2445

I hope this has helped you.
Good luck on your journey.

Name: _____    Hector Suco    Date: _____

# Marriage

This worksheet can be filled out by you alone or with your spouse. It is up to your discretion.

1. How long have you been married? _____

2. How would you rate your marriage?

```
<---|-----------------------|-----------------------|--->
    0                       5                       10
```

3. Why did you give your marriage that rating?

_____

_____

4. Is this the first marriage for both of you?
☐ Yes
☐ No: Explain.

_____

_____

5. In what ways can your marriage improve?

_____

_____

6. Have you ever been to a marriage counselor?

☐ Yes: Why? How often have you gone?

_____

☐ No: Would you ever go see a marriage counselor? Why or why not?

_____

7. What are some of your goals as a married couple?

_____

_____

_____

_____

8. Have you ever been romantically attracted to someone else? If so, explain.

_____

_____

9. Have you ever been tempted by someone else to betray/cheat on your spouse?

_____

_____

10. Have you ever betrayed/cheated on your spouse? Has your spouse ever betrayed/cheated on you?

_____

_____

_____

_____

# Finances

11. You and your partner have:
    - ☐ Joint Bank Account
    - ☐ Separate Bank Accounts
    - ☐ Both Joint & Separate Bank Accounts

11A: Do you have a secret account that your spouse doesn't know about?

☐ No

☐ Yes: Explain: _____

12. Have you and your partner ever over-drafted? If so, why?

_____

_____

13. Do you and your partner have savings or investment accounts? Explain.

_____

_____

14. Do you and your spouse have debt? How much? How are you handling your debt?

_____

_____

15. What are your financial goals as a married couple?

_____

_____

# Children

16. Do you have children?

☐ No

☐ Yes: How many? _____ How old are they? _____ If your children are over 18, are they still living at home? _____

17. Do you want (more) children?

☐ No

☐ Yes: How many (more)? _____ By When? _____

# Social Life

18. How would you describe your social life with your spouse?

_____

_____

19. How often do you go out with other friends without your spouse?

_____

_____

20. Are there any hobbies or activities you do together?

_____

# Religion

21. What religion do you and your spouse practice?

_____

_____

22. How important is religion in your marriage?

_____

_____

# Sex

23. Are you content with your sex life?

☐ Yes

☐ No: Why not?

_____

_____

24. How often do you have sex? _____

25. Do you want more or less sex? _____

25A. Why do you feel this way?

_____

_____

# Values

For #26 – 34, circle 1 – 10 based on how important each is in your marriage with 1 being the least important and 10 being most important. Then, write how important your partner feels that they are.

**26. Respect, Honesty & Trust**            1   2   3   4   5   6   7   8   9   10

_____

_____

**27. Life Goals, Lifestyle**            1   2   3   4   5   6   7   8   9   10

_____

_____

**28. Career**            1   2   3   4   5   6   7   8   9   10

_____

_____

**29. Religion**            1   2   3   4   5   6   7   8   9   10

_____

_____

**30. Commitment/Loyalty**            1   2   3   4   5   6   7   8   9   10

_____

_____

31. Selflessness/Sacrifice          1  2  3  4  5  6  7  8  9  10

_____

_____

32. Patience/Forgiveness            1  2  3  4  5  6  7  8  9  10

_____

_____

33. Children                        1  2  3  4  5  6  7  8  9  10

_____

_____

34. Family                          1  2  3  4  5  6  7  8  9  10

_____

_____

35. Abuse                           1  2  3  4  5  6  7  8  9  10
(verbal, emotional, physical, substance, alcohol)

_____

_____

Name: _____  Hector Suco  Date: _____

# Marriage

This worksheet can be filled out by you alone or with your spouse. It is up to your discretion.

1. How long have you been married? _____

2. How would you rate your marriage?

```
<---+----------------------------+----------------------------+-->
    0                            5                            10
```

3. Why did you give your marriage that rating?

_____

_____

4. Is this the first marriage for both of you?
   ☐ Yes
   ☐ No: Explain.

_____

_____

5. In what ways can your marriage improve?

_____

_____

6. Have you ever been to a marriage counselor?

☐ Yes: Why? How often have you gone?

_____

☐ No: Would you ever go see a marriage counselor? Why or why not?

_____

7. What are some of your goals as a married couple?

_____

_____

_____

_____

8. Have you ever been romantically attracted to someone else? If so, explain.

_____

_____

9. Have you ever been tempted by someone else to betray/cheat on your spouse?

_____

_____

10. Have you ever betrayed/cheated on your spouse? Has your spouse ever betrayed/cheated on you?

_____

_____

_____

_____

# Finances

11. You and your partner have:
- ☐ Joint Bank Account
- ☐ Separate Bank Accounts
- ☐ Both Joint & Separate Bank Accounts

11A: Do you have a secret account that your spouse doesn't know about?

☐ No

☐ Yes: Explain: _____

12. Have you and your partner ever over-drafted? If so, why?

_____

_____

13. Do you and your partner have savings or investment accounts? Explain.

_____

_____

14. Do you and your spouse have debt? How much? How are you handling your debt?

_____

_____

15. What are your financial goals as a married couple?

_____

_____

# Children

16. Do you have children?

☐ No

☐ Yes: How many? _____ How old are they? _____ If your children are over 18, are they still living at home? _____

17. Do you want (more) children?

☐ No

☐ Yes: How many (more)? _____ By When? _____

# Social Life

18. How would you describe your social life with your spouse?

_____

_____

19. How often do you go out with other friends without your spouse?

_____

_____

20. Are there any hobbies or activities you do together?

_____

# Religion

21. What religion do you and your spouse practice?

_____

_____

22. How important is religion in your marriage?

_____

_____

# Sex

23. Are you content with your sex life?

☐ Yes

☐ No: Why not?

_____

_____

24. How often do you have sex? _____

25. Do you want more or less sex? _____

25A. Why do you feel this way?

_____

_____

# Values

For #26 – 34, circle 1 – 10 based on how important each is in your marriage with 1 being the least important and 10 being most important. Then, write how important your partner feels that they are.

26. Respect, Honesty & Trust     1  2  3  4  5  6  7  8  9  10

_____

_____

27. Life Goals, Lifestyle     1  2  3  4  5  6  7  8  9  10

_____

_____

28. Career     1  2  3  4  5  6  7  8  9  10

_____

_____

29. Religion     1  2  3  4  5  6  7  8  9  10

_____

_____

30. Commitment/Loyalty     1  2  3  4  5  6  7  8  9  10

_____

_____

31. Selflessness/Sacrifice             1   2   3   4   5   6   7   8   9   10

_____

_____

32. Patience/Forgiveness               1   2   3   4   5   6   7   8   9   10

_____

_____

33. Children                           1   2   3   4   5   6   7   8   9   10

_____

_____

34. Family                             1   2   3   4   5   6   7   8   9   10

_____

_____

35. Abuse                              1   2   3   4   5   6   7   8   9   10
(verbal, emotional, physical, substance, alcohol)

_____

_____

# Marriage Worksheet Guide

2. One's answers will never be the same from time to time. Marriage has its ups and downs. If your spouse were to answer this question in secret, would your answers match theirs?

3. Rating of 1-3: Explicitly write down your marital problems from the biggest to the smallest. What needs the most work and how are the both of you going to bring that number up?
Rating of 4-7: An average marriage is okay, but it could be better. Write down the good and the bad. What is working and not working in your marriage. How can it be better?
Rating of 8-9: Excellent. Write down what's working. Also, write down the issues that are stopping your marriage from becoming a 10.
Rating of 10: Excellent job. What is it about your marriage that makes you feel this way?

4. What did you or your partner learn from the last long-term relationship you had? How can that help you both grow together? How can those lessons help you in this marriage?

5. No marriage is perfect. Whether it is something small or big, write how you think your marriage can improve. Do not write how much your spouse needs to change. If you have married your spouse with the intention of changing them, you are in for a rude awakening. You will have to make adjustments too if you want your marriage to work. How you will do that is up to you and your spouse.

6. Marriage counselors have studied relationships and what makes them tick. They went to school for it. They are a vast reservoir of knowledge and well-founded advice for any couple. My wife and I have gone to a marriage counselor. We didn't have any serious problems; we went as a marriage checkup, which is something I recommend for all married couples. You do not necessarily need to see a counselor, but a sit down and talk every once in a while about where you've been, and where you are going, and what problems you are having and how to solve them. Reflecting on your relationship is healthy and is almost sure-fire way to improve it.

7. Examples include:

| Better/More Sex | Better/More Communication | Get out of debt | Better social life / Go out more | Have children |
|---|---|---|---|---|
| Do different things/Spice up | More Dates | Save more money | Say "I love you" more often | Better sense of family time |
| Work less | More time together | Add more romance. | Share chores | More intimacy |

8. Seeing someone and thinking they're attractive is bound to happen – we are human. However, if you find yourself thinking about that person beyond initial attraction, you may need to check your priorities. Does this person mean more to you than your spouse? Are you willing to risk your relationship for them?

9. Sometimes we have thoughts we do not think we should, like what it would be like to cheat on a partner. Now, thoughts are one thing, but actions are another entirely. Think of your actions this way: *Would I be upset if I found out my spouse was doing this?* If you would be upset, you probably shouldn't do it yourself.

10. Please use the Romantic Betrayed and/or Romantic Betrayer Worksheet.

11. Having joint or separate bank accounts is a choice that could be different for every couple. Talk it out with your partner. If you find yourself on the fence about which road to take, you might want to seek the advice of a financial advisor.

11A. Honesty really is the best policy. If there is a secret account, why does it exist? Why can't you tell your partner about it? Think about telling them about it. Continuing to lie will only breed mistrust.

12. Over-drafting is not fun. Most banks charge you for over drafting your account. Have your safe fallbacks so the landing won't be so hard. Work together as a team to make sure you always have money in the bank.

13. Examples of savings accounts include:

| Emergency | Vacation | Children | Projects | Hobbies |
|---|---|---|---|---|
| House Expenses | Car Expenses | Retirement | | |

Go see a financial advisor to start investing.

14. Having debt is not a good feeling. It is like a dark cloud hanging over you. You cringe each time that bill comes in the mail. There are many ways to cut debt like debt stacking, using a debt relief program, or consolidating your debt into one payment. Utilize a financial advisor as needed.

15. Examples include:

| Get out of / Lower debt | Invest (more) | Save money | Create cushion |
|---|---|---|---|

16. What role do your children play in your marriage? Do they enhance your marriage or do you fight about them with your partner?

17. Are you ready to take on the responsibilities of being a parent? Are you emotionally and financially ready to have another child?

18. Being social is a healthy part of being a well-rounded individual. A night out on the town, a nice restaurant, a game night with friends, a sports event, concerts, etc. These are all great date ideas – get out there and have some fun with your partner!

19. If one spouse cannot go out without the other, there is a trust issue. Why can't they go out without you? Have then done something in the past to make you not trust them? Is it you who cannot go out alone? Why do you think your partner feels the need to go everywhere with you? Talk this out.

20. Having common hobbies is always a plus – it means more quality time together.

21. Do you and your spouse practice the same religion? Different religions? Do you or your spouse practice no religion? If you and your spouse do not practice the same religion, have you decided under which religion you will raise your children?

22. If you and your spouse have the same answer, then you have nothing to discuss. If you have different opinions, sit down and chat about them. Can you both live together practicing different religions?

23. If you picked yes, you are on the right track. If you picked no, write down why and how would you like your sex life to improve.

24. This number depends on each marriage. For some marriages, it is daily. For other marriages, it is weekly. However, not being intimate with your partner for long stretches of time could be a red flag. Talk to your spouse and try to initiate intimacy. If it happens, fantastic! If it doesn't, it may be time to talk.

25. "More" would be the answer for most, but what does that entail? What else needs to happen for the both of you to have sex more often? What gets your spouse in the mood? Are you children an obstacle to overcome? If the amount is not the issue, try to find the solutions that will work for you and your spouse.

26. How important is respect in your marriage? How honest do you expect each other to be in this marriage? How upset would you be if you found out your spouse lied? What if it was only a white lie?

27. Yours and your partner's goals do not have to be exactly the same, but they should at least compliment each other. If you want five kids and they want two, see if you can compromise. If they want to take up tandem skydiving and you do not like the idea of jumping out of planes, just talk to them about it.

28. The issue may not be the occupation itself, but the pay and/or lifestyle. Would you be okay with someone that has a job requiring them to work at night and sleep during the day? Firefighters are gone for 24 to 48 hours at a time. Police officers put their life on the line every day. Do you support each other and your careers?

29. Success stories of couples from different religions exist all over the world. The difference is a hurdle to jump over, not a mountain to climb. How do you and your spouse see it? The fact that you are married shows that your relationship is at least a little more important than your need to have a religious marriage. How important is religion in your marriage? Do you pray together? Apart?

30. What does loyalty mean to you? How important is it that your partner be "loyal"? How important are promises in your relationship? What happens if one of you breaks a promise to the other?

31. Marriage is not always 50/50, and the difference is not usually because one partner is not trying. Many things, like depression, can cause partners to be able to put less of themselves into their relationship. How okay are you with doing 80% on the days when your spouse can only do 20%?

32. Your partner has and will continue to make mistakes, as will you. If you would like your partner to be patient with you and forgive you, you should repay the favor.

33. Having children is a common life goal. How many children do you want? How important is it for you to have biological children (flesh and blood)? If one of you is infertile, will you adopt? Would you be willing to spend the thousands of dollars needed for in vitro fertilization?

34. How important do you feel the family you do not live with are? Do you need to visit once a week, or is a call enough? Do you have a good relationship with your parents and siblings? Does your spouse?

35. You need to be clear with your partner about what is acceptable and what is not. Physical, verbal, or psychological abuse should be a deal breaker in **any** type of relationship. Would you be okay with your partner taking drugs? Would you mind if they had a drink or two or three every day? How about smoking cigarettes?

I hope this has helped you.
Good luck on your journey.

Name: _____    Hector Suco    Date: _____

# Sex

1. Age: _____

2. What is your relationship status? (Select One)

|   | Status | Definition |
|---|---|---|
| ☐ | Single | Not dating or talking to anyone |
| ☐ | Dating | Going out and spending time with different people |
| ☐ | In A Relationship | "Official" Relationship, Engaged, or Married |

3. At what age did you lose your virginity? _____

☐ I am a virgin (Continue and stop at 3A)

3A. At what age would you like to lose your virginity and why? Have you chosen to remain abstinent for any specific reason? _____

_____

4. How many sexual partners have you had? _____

5. Do you regret any past experiences you have had in your sex life? If so, explain: _____

_____

6. List the reason(s) you have sex.

|   |   |   |   |   |
|---|---|---|---|---|
|   |   |   |   |   |
|   |   |   |   |   |
|   |   |   |   |   |

7. From a 0 – 10, how satisfying is it when you have sex with someone/your partner?

```
0                              5                              10
```

8. How important is sex in your life/relationship?

_____

_____

_____

_____

9. Do you speak about sex with your partner to improve/ make the sex better? Why or why not?

_____

_____

_____

_____

Name: _____  Hector Suco  Date: _____

# Sex

1. Age: _____

2. What is your relationship status? (Select One)

|   | Status | Definition |
|---|--------|------------|
| ☐ | Single | Not dating or talking to anyone |
| ☐ | Dating | Going out and spending time with different people |
| ☐ | In A Relationship | "Official" Relationship, Engaged, or Married |

3. At what age did you lose your virginity? _____

☐ I am a virgin (Continue and stop at 3A)

3A. At what age would you like to lose your virginity and why? Have you chosen to remain abstinent for any specific reason? _____

_____

4. How many sexual partners have you had? _____

5. Do you regret any past experiences you have had in your sex life? If so, explain: _____

_____

6. List the reason(s) you have sex.

|   |   |   |   |   |
|---|---|---|---|---|
|   |   |   |   |   |
|   |   |   |   |   |
|   |   |   |   |   |

7. From a 0 – 10, how satisfying is it when you have sex with someone/your partner?

```
0                            5                           10
```

8. How important is sex in your life/relationship?

_____

_____

_____

_____

9. Do you speak about sex with your partner to improve/ make the sex better? Why or why not?

_____

_____

_____

_____

Name: _____   Hector Suco   Date: _____

# Sex

1. Age: _____

2. What is your relationship status? (Select One)

|   | **Status** | **Definition** |
|---|---|---|
| ☐ | Single | Not dating or talking to anyone |
| ☐ | Dating | Going out and spending time with different people |
| ☐ | In A Relationship | "Official" Relationship, Engaged, or Married |

3. At what age did you lose your virginity? _____

☐ I'm a virgin (Continue and stop at 3A)

3A. At what age would you like to lose your virginity and why? Have you chosen to remain abstinent for any specific reason? _____

_____

4. How many sexual partners have you had?

5. Do you regret any past experiences you have had in your sex life? If so, explain: _____

_____

6. List the reason(s) you have sex.

|   |   |   |   |   |
|---|---|---|---|---|
|   |   |   |   |   |
|   |   |   |   |   |
|   |   |   |   |   |

7. From a 0 – 10, how satisfying is it when you have sex with someone/your partner?

```
0                              5                              10
```

8. How important is sex in your life/relationship?

_____
_____
_____
_____

9. Do you speak about sex with your partner to improve/ make the sex better? Why or why not?

_____
_____
_____
_____

# Sex Worksheet Guide

4. On Urban Dictionary, there is a "Rule of Three" entry that states "When asking someone about the number of sexual partners they've had, multiply a woman's answer by 3 because ladies do not want to seem like the slut. When a man answers, divide his number by 3 because he wants to seem like a player."
This was confirmed when a study polled over 1,300 women. They were asked what lies they most told when in a relationship. 52% responded with the number of previous partners. Starting any kind of relationship on a lie is not a good sign. Try to be honest with yourself and your partner.

5. We all have bad experiences - they cannot all be 10 out of 10. However, you shouldn't let bad times in the past make you jaded. Live through your mistakes and learn from them. Use the space to write out any other bad experiences you have had and start the process of getting better.

6. Examples include:

| | | |
|---|---|---|
| Pleasure | To get pregnant | Better connection with partner/intimacy |
| Everyone else is doing it | I want to keep my partner happy/satisfied | Revenge/To make someone jealous |
| Stress relief | I want my partner to love me | It fulfills my want to control |
| Money/Gifts | Distraction | Addiction |

7. 0-4: Try to communicate more with your partner(s) about what your likes and dislikes are. Sex is a two way street and the goal is for both streets to merge at the same time and head in the same direction.

5-7: It is there, but it needs work. Be sure to continue to communicate with your partner about your likes and dislikes. Try having an open dialogue about this - your partner knowing what you like is the only way for them to give that to you.

8-10: Good job. Continue doing what you're doing.

8. Sex may be important to some, but not others. Where would you rank sex on the list of priorities in your life? Too much or too little sex is not good. Like anything else in life, you need a balance.

9. Communication is one of the roots of a relationship. Knowing what your partner, likes and dislikes are, and vice versa, will make sex that much better for both of you.

I hope this has helped you.
Good luck on your journey.

Name: _____   Hector Suco   Date: _____

# Relationship Finances

This worksheet is for any couples and their finances.

1. Which describes yours and your partner's bank account(s)?
- ☐ Joint Account
- ☐ Separate Accounts
- ☐ Both Joint & Separate Accounts

1A: Is there a secret account involved?

☐ No

☐ Yes: Explain: _____

2. Do you and your partner have savings accounts?

☐ Yes. What are you saving for? _____

☐ No. Explain: _____

3. Do you and your partner have investment accounts?

☐ Yes. Explain: _____

☐ No. Explain: _____

4. Do you and your spouse have debt? How much? How are you handling your debt?

_____

_____

5. What are your financial goals as a couple?

_____

_____

6. What are your individual financial goals?

_____

_____

7. Have you and your partner ever over-drafted? If so, why?

_____

_____

7A. What are the steps you are taking to make sure it does not happen again?

_____

_____

8. Which one of you is the…

…spender? _____

…saver? _____

9. How often do you talk about your finances as a couple?

_____

10. Who handles the finances in your relationship?

_____

11. Are you satisfied with your current income?

☐ Yes

☐ No. Explain: _____

_____

12. Do you think you are in need of more income?

_____

_____

13. If something were to happen to you or your partner, how would the other be financially impacted?

_____

_____

14. How would you rate your financial situation?

```
←|―――――――――――――|―――――――――――――|→
0              5             10
```

15. Why do you feel this way?

_____

_____

16. Is there anything you think can be done to improve your finances? If so, what?

_____

_____

Name: _____   Hector Suco   Date: _____

# Relationship Finances

This worksheet is for any couples and their finances.

1. Which describes yours and your partner's bank account(s)?
   - ☐ Joint Account
   - ☐ Separate Accounts
   - ☐ Both Joint & Separate Accounts

1A: Is there a secret account involved?

☐ No

☐ Yes: Explain: _____

2. Do you and your partner have savings accounts?

☐ Yes. What are you saving for? _____

☐ No. Explain: _____

3. Do you and your partner have investment accounts?

☐ Yes. Explain: _____

☐ No. Explain: _____

4. Do you and your spouse have debt? How much? How are you handling your debt?

_____

_____

5. What are your financial goals as a couple?

_____

_____

6. What are your individual financial goals?

_____

_____

7. Have you and your partner ever over-drafted? If so, why?

_____

_____

7A. What are the steps you are taking to make sure it does not happen again?

_____

_____

8. Which one of you is the…

…spender? _____

…saver? _____

9. How often do you talk about your finances as a couple?

_____

10. Who handles the finances in your relationship?

_____

11. Are you satisfied with your current income?

☐ Yes

☐ No. Explain: _____

_____

12. Do you think you are in need of more income?

_____
_____

13. If something were to happen to you or your partner, how would the other be financially impacted?

_____
_____

14. How would you rate your financial situation?

```
←+----------------+----------------+→
0                 5                10
```

15. Why do you feel this way?

_____
_____

16. Is there anything you think can be done to improve your finances? If so, what?

_____
_____

Name: _____    Hector Suco    Date: _____

# Relationship Finances

This worksheet is for any couples and their finances.

1. Which describes yours and your partner's bank account(s)?
   - ☐ Joint Account
   - ☐ Separate Accounts
   - ☐ Both Joint & Separate Accounts

1A: Is there a secret account involved?

- ☐ No

- ☐ Yes: Explain: _____

2. Do you and your partner have savings accounts?

- ☐ Yes. What are you saving for? _____

- ☐ No. Explain: _____

3. Do you and your partner have investment accounts?

- ☐ Yes. Explain: _____

- ☐ No. Explain: _____

4. Do you and your spouse have debt? How much? How are you handling your debt?

_____

_____

5. What are your financial goals as a couple?

_____

_____

6. What are your individual financial goals?

_____

_____

7. Have you and your partner ever over-drafted? If so, why?

_____

_____

7A. What are the steps you are taking to make sure it does not happen again?

_____

_____

8. Which one of you is the…

…spender? _____

…saver? _____

9. How often do you talk about your finances as a couple?

_____

10. Who handles the finances in your relationship?

_____

11. Are you satisfied with your current income?

☐ Yes

☐ No. Explain: _____

_____

12. Do you think you are in need of more income?

_____

_____

13. If something were to happen to you or your partner, how would the other be financially impacted?

_____

_____

14. How would you rate your financial situation?

0 —————————————— 5 —————————————— 10

15. Why do you feel this way?

_____

_____

16. Is there anything you think can be done to improve your finances? If so, what?

_____

_____

# Relationship Finances Worksheet Guide

1. Whether to have a joint account, separate accounts, or both is one decision that all couples need to make for themselves. If you are not sure whether you should have one or multiple accounts, write the pros and cons of each and come to an agreement. It is fine to have multiple accounts if your finances allow it.

1A. Honesty really is the best policy. Hiding money is a big deal. Do not risk your partner's trust over some extra cash.

If you're keeping some money aside to buy a gift, just keep it in your bank account. Let your partner know that you want to save a certain amount of money for later. Do not keep secrets. It is a bad idea.

2. Examples of savings accounts include:

| Emergency | Vacation | Children | Projects | Hobbies |
|---|---|---|---|---|
| House Expenses | Car Expenses | Retirement | Education | Miscellaneous |

If you and your partner do not have savings accounts, it is time to start. This is the principle of "pay yourself first." Essentially, if all you pay is bills and you do not save for yourself, you will always be broke. It is time to start saving.

3. If you are working hard for your money, then your money should be working for you. Investing is one of the steps in the long road toward becoming financially independent. To find what suits your needs, you should seek the advice of a financial advisor.

4. There are many ways to cut debt like debt stacking, using a debt relief program, or consolidating your debt into one payment. Use a financial advisor as needed.

5. & 6. Examples include:

| Get out of / Lower debt | Invest (more) | Save money | Create cushion |
| --- | --- | --- | --- |
| Buying a home | Vacations (more) | Being financially independent | Reaching your retirement goal |
| Helping loved ones | Special events | Living your dream | Miscellaneous |

7. & 7A. Over drafting is not fun. Most banks charge you for over drafting your account. Some banks allow you to have a credit card on file to prevent you from over drafting by charging the card. Banks also have notices in place that lets customers know when their bank accounts fall below a certain threshold. Find a threshold that gives both of you enough time to react to the situation. Take advantage of this and any other service. Have your safe fallbacks so the landing won't be so hard. Work together as a team to make sure you always have money in the bank.

8. Being honest with each other and yourself is the best way to do anything. Secondly, being supportive of each other will make any process much simpler. Jan D. Anderson, Ph.D., performed a study in 2000 that indicated statistically significant relationships between financial problems and divorce.
Source: https://digitalcommons.usu.edu/etd/2445

Carolina Bermudez, a celebrity personality, once said on-air that her husband would need to be making $250,000 a year to support her spending habits. Look down the road and make a plan that you both can agree on when it comes to finances and your budget. It might be frustrating and/or tedious, but you need to be constantly talking about finances with your partner. As life changes, your finances will change. Ideally, if you talk about your finances once a year, you and your partner should be on the right track. Take a couple of hours to hash everything out, including your budget, spending habits, financial goals, retirement plans, etc.

9. & 10. This decision has to be made within each couple. Some couples might decide that they are both responsible for handling the bills. Other couples may have one partner who may be better with money that offers to take charge of the finances. Whichever way you and your partner decide, make sure you make the decision together.

11. Most couples will answer no, unless you are in a place where you are comfortable. In some cases, a couple definitely needs more income. In some cases, certain lifestyles need to change to fit the couple's needs (not wants). This question is here so that you can open an honest dialogue about your finances with your partner.

12. If you think you need more money, first ask yourself and your partner why. Then think of ways to change your current income. Make a list and write down the pros and cons to each option.

13. If you and your partner do not have insurance, would one of you dying cause the other extreme financial strain? Would they be able to pay for your expenses and then survive on their own? Do you both have life insurance? You might want to look into it now, as it gets more expensive as you age. If a life insurance policy has, for example, $300,000, your policy will determine how that money is distributed. The money can be dispersed all at once. The money can be dispersed throughout time (over 20 years, your partner would receive $1,250 a month). Some of the money can be dispersed now (for funeral costs), and then distributed over time. If you do have one, you need to be aware of how your policy works.

14. & 15. If you and your partner answered this question separately, would the answers match? Are you living within your means? Are you being honest with your partner? If your score is low, it does not mean the world is ending. It just means…

16. …you need to put the time and effort to work on your financial plan together.

I hope this has helped you.
Good luck on your journey.

Name: _____        Hector Suco        Date: _____

# Relationship Checkup

1. How is this worksheet going to be filled out?
☐ Alone
☐ With my partner

2. How long have you two been together? _____

3. Have there been any breaks in your relationship in the last year?
☐ Yes
☐ No

3A. Have there been any breaks in your relationship since it started?
☐ Yes
☐ No

4. When was the last relationship checkup, if any? _____

5. With 1 being the worst and 10 being the best, how would you rate your relationship…

…since the beginning?

0 — 5 — 10

…in the last year?

0 — 5 — 10

…right now?

0 — 5 — 10

6. List the issues in your relationship that need work. What causes the arguments/fights?

|  |  |  |  |
|--|--|--|--|
|  |  |  |  |
|  |  |  |  |
|  |  |  |  |

7. With the issues stated in #6, write your opinion about the problems and possible compromises **you** are willing to make.

_____

_____

_____

_____

8. Write down a promise/contract for yourself in regards to the compromises/changes/adjustments you will make in order to better your relationship.

_____

_____

_____

_____

9. Are there any personality traits that are difficult for one or the other partner to accept?

_____

_____

_____

_____

Name: _____      Hector Suco      Date: _____

# Relationship Checkup

1. How is this worksheet going to be filled out?
☐ Alone
☐ With my partner

2. How long have you two been together? _____

3. Have there been any breaks in your relationship in the last year?
☐ Yes
☐ No

3A. Have there been any breaks in your relationship since it started?
☐ Yes
☐ No

4. When was the last relationship checkup, if any? _____

5. With 1 being the worst and 10 being the best, how would you rate your relationship…

…since the beginning?

0 — 5 — 10

…in the last year?

0 — 5 — 10

…right now?

0 — 5 — 10

6. List the issues in your relationship that need work. What causes the arguments/fights?

|  |  |  |  |
|---|---|---|---|
|  |  |  |  |
|  |  |  |  |
|  |  |  |  |

7. With the issues stated in #6, write your opinion about the problems and possible compromises **you** are willing to make.

_____
_____
_____
_____
_____

8. Write down a promise/contract for yourself in regards to the compromises/changes/adjustments you will make in order to better your relationship.

_____
_____
_____
_____
_____

9. Are there any personality traits that are difficult for one or the other partner to accept?

_____
_____
_____
_____

Name: _____  Hector Suco  Date: _____

# Relationship Checkup

1. How is this worksheet going to be filled out?
☐ Alone
☐ With my partner

2. How long have you two been together? _____

3. Have there been any breaks in your relationship in the last year?
☐ Yes
☐ No

3A. Have there been any breaks in your relationship since it started?
☐ Yes
☐ No

4. When was the last relationship checkup, if any? _____

5. With 1 being the worst and 10 being the best, how would you rate your relationship…

…since the beginning?

0 — 5 — 10

…in the last year?

0 — 5 — 10

…right now?

0 — 5 — 10

6. List the issues in your relationship that need work. What causes the arguments/fights?

|  |  |  |  |
|---|---|---|---|
|  |  |  |  |
|  |  |  |  |
|  |  |  |  |

7. With the issues stated in #6, write your opinion about the problems and possible compromises **you** are willing to make.

_____

_____

_____

_____

_____


8. Write down a promise/contract for yourself in regards to the compromises/changes/adjustments you will make in order to better your relationship.

_____

_____

_____

_____

_____


9. Are there any personality traits that are difficult for one or the other partner to accept?

_____

_____

_____

_____

Name: _____  Hector Suco  Date: _____

# Relationship Checkup

1. How is this worksheet going to be filled out?
   ☐ Alone
   ☐ With my partner

2. How long have you two been together? _____

3. Have there been any breaks in your relationship in the last year?
   ☐ Yes
   ☐ No

3A. Have there been any breaks in your relationship since it started?
   ☐ Yes
   ☐ No

4. When was the last relationship checkup, if any? _____

5. With 1 being the worst and 10 being the best, how would you rate your relationship…

…since the beginning?

0 — 5 — 10

…in the last year?

0 — 5 — 10

…right now?

0 — 5 — 10

6. List the issues in your relationship that need work. What causes the arguments/fights?

| | | | |
|---|---|---|---|
| | | | |
| | | | |
| | | | |

7. With the issues stated in #6, write your opinion about the problems and possible compromises **you** are willing to make.

_____

_____

_____

_____

8. Write down a promise/contract for yourself in regards to the compromises/changes/adjustments you will make in order to better your relationship.

_____

_____

_____

_____

9. Are there any personality traits that are difficult for one or the other partner to accept?

_____

_____

_____

_____

Name: _____     Hector Suco     Date: _____

# Relationship Checkup

1. How is this worksheet going to be filled out?
 ☐ Alone
 ☐ With my partner

2. How long have you two been together? _____

3. Have there been any breaks in your relationship in the last year?
 ☐ Yes
 ☐ No

3A. Have there been any breaks in your relationship since it started?
 ☐ Yes
 ☐ No

4. When was the last relationship checkup, if any? _____

5. With 1 being the worst and 10 being the best, how would you rate your relationship…

…since the beginning?

0 — 5 — 10

…in the last year?

0 — 5 — 10

…right now?

0 — 5 — 10

6. List the issues in your relationship that need work. What causes the arguments/fights?

|  |  |  |  |
|--|--|--|--|
|  |  |  |  |
|  |  |  |  |
|  |  |  |  |

7. With the issues stated in #6, write your opinion about the problems and possible compromises **you** are willing to make.

_____

_____

_____

_____

8. Write down a promise/contract for yourself in regards to the compromises/changes/adjustments you will make in order to better your relationship.

_____

_____

_____

_____

9. Are there any personality traits that are difficult for one or the other partner to accept?

_____

_____

_____

_____

# Relationship Checkup Worksheet Guide

1. You choose how to fill this worksheet out. Filling this worksheet out together may help your communication with your partner. If you fill out this worksheet alone, sharing your answers with your partner may also help with communication.

2. Any relationship length can benefit from a checkup.

3. Yes: What caused the separation? How long did it last? Why did you two get back together? Were there any compromises that were made? What steps will you and your partner make to make sure it does not happen again? Please use the Break-Up Worksheet or the Marriage Separation Worksheet to go more in-depth.

4. Just like the body needs checkups, relationships need checkups, too. If there are any issues on or under the surface, they can be brought out during the checkup and, hopefully, be resolved.

5. Rating your relationship in its different stages is important. It shows where you've been, where you are now, and can give clues as to where your relationship is going. If your rating for one stage is greater compared to any of the other stages, try to figure out why that is. Maybe you stopped doing something a while ago that helped your relationship, even something as simple as buying your partner flowers once a month. If that made your relationship better, you should start doing it again!

6. Examples include:

| Lack of communication | Little to no romance | Financial problems | Nagging |
|---|---|---|---|
| Trust issues | Little to no intimacy | Disagreements | Not 50/50 |
| Values | Little to no sex | Children | Religion |

7. *The Onion*, a satire news organization, has an article about blame being the fastest human reflex, comparing the act of blaming someone to blinking and flinching. Changes to the "brain's neural pathways" have allowed "for a nearly instantaneous transition between perceiving a problem and condemning someone else for causing it." They end the article stating that the "accepting responsibility reflex" has been suppressed and may leave the human race forever. Although comedic, the article suggests that our current society likes to blame others and we dislike taking personal responsibility for certain problems. That is why for #7, I ask what compromises **you** will make in order for this relationship to get better.

8. You have to look deep inside yourself and consciously chose how you will change/adjust/compromise. I want you to write a contract to yourself or to your partner addressing how you will work to better your relationship.

9. Examples include:

| Selfish | Rude | Arrogant | Untrustworthy |
|---|---|---|---|
| Intense | Angry | Biased | Bad Tempered |
| Boring | Cold | Conceited | Cruel |
| Deceiving | Dishonest | Disrespectful | Distant |
| Egotistical | Envy | Immature | Jealous |
| Lazy | Mean | Nasty | Self-Centered |
| Secretive | Unappreciative | Uncooperative | Unkind |

I hope this has helped you.
Good luck on your journey.

Name: _____    Hector Suco    Date: _____

# Honesty Hour

"Honesty is the best policy," rings true especially for relationships. If you or your partner have issues and are holding them in, no matter how small, they can add a weight of stress in the relationship. Take one hour, every week or every month, to sit down with your partner and hash out all of the issues you have with them and them with you. Provide your partner with the same worksheet. You both will never agree on everything, but when it is out in the open, both partners will feel vindicated that their voice was heard. Practice this enough so that you will not need a worksheet and you will just be honest with each other all of the time!

1. List all of the issues that you have held in and not told your partner. If one issue is greatly important, use as many numbers as needed.

1. _____

2. _____

3. _____

4. _____

5. _____

6. _____

7. _____

8. _____

9. _____

10. _____

On the next page, you or your partner will write their response on the first line along with any and all possible solution(s) to each issue on the second line.

2. Either record your partner's response or have them respond to each issue. Use the second line provided to write any and all possible solutions to the issue.

1. _____

   _____

2. _____

   _____

3. _____

   _____

4. _____

   _____

5. _____

   _____

6. _____

   _____

7. _____

   _____

8. _____

   _____

9. _____

   _____

10. _____

    _____

Name: _____   Hector Suco   Date: _____

# Honesty Hour

"Honesty is the best policy," rings true especially for relationships. If you or your partner have issues and are holding them in, no matter how small, they can add a weight of stress in the relationship. Take one hour, every week or every month, to sit down with your partner and hash out all of the issues you have with them and them with you. Provide your partner with the same worksheet. You both will never agree on everything, but when it is out in the open, both partners will feel vindicated that their voice was heard. Practice this enough so that you will not need a worksheet and you will just be honest with each other all of the time!

1. List all of the issues that you have held in and not told your partner. If one issue is greatly important, use as many numbers as needed.

1. _____

2. _____

3. _____

4. _____

5. _____

6. _____

7. _____

8. _____

9. _____

10. _____

On the next page, you or your partner will write their response on the first line along with any and all possible solution(s) to each issue on the second line.

2. Either record your partner's response or have them respond to each issue. Use the second line provided to write any and all possible solutions to the issue.

1. _____

   _____

2. _____

   _____

3. _____

   _____

4. _____

   _____

5. _____

   _____

6. _____

   _____

7. _____

   _____

8. _____

   _____

9. _____

   _____

10. _____

    _____

Name: _____     Hector Suco     Date: _____

# Honesty Hour

"Honesty is the best policy," rings true especially for relationships. If you or your partner have issues and are holding them in, no matter how small, they can add a weight of stress in the relationship. Take one hour, every week or every month, to sit down with your partner and hash out all of the issues you have with them and them with you. Provide your partner with the same worksheet. You both will never agree on everything, but when it is out in the open, both partners will feel vindicated that their voice was heard. Practice this enough so that you will not need a worksheet and you will just be honest with each other all of the time!

1. List all of the issues that you have held in and not told your partner. If one issue is greatly important, use as many numbers as needed.

1. _____

2. _____

3. _____

4. _____

5. _____

6. _____

7. _____

8. _____

9. _____

10. _____

On the next page, you or your partner will write their response on the first line along with any and all possible solution(s) to each issue on the second line.

2. Either record your partner's response or have them respond to each issue. Use the second line provided to write any and all possible solutions to the issue.

1. _____

   _____

2. _____

   _____

3. _____

   _____

4. _____

   _____

5. _____

   _____

6. _____

   _____

7. _____

   _____

8. _____

   _____

9. _____

   _____

10. _____

    _____

Name: _____    Hector Suco    Date: _____

# Honesty Hour

"Honesty is the best policy," rings true especially for relationships. If you or your partner have issues and are holding them in, no matter how small, they can add a weight of stress in the relationship. Take one hour, every week or every month, to sit down with your partner and hash out all of the issues you have with them and them with you. Provide your partner with the same worksheet. You both will never agree on everything, but when it is out in the open, both partners will feel vindicated that their voice was heard. Practice this enough so that you will not need a worksheet and you will just be honest with each other all of the time!

1. List all of the issues that you have held in and not told your partner. If one issue is greatly important, use as many numbers as needed.

1. _____

2. _____

3. _____

4. _____

5. _____

6. _____

7. _____

8. _____

9. _____

10. _____

On the next page, you or your partner will write their response on the first line along with any and all possible solution(s) to each issue on the second line.

2. Either record your partner's response or have them respond to each issue. Use the second line provided to write any and all possible solutions to the issue.

1. _____

   _____

2. _____

   _____

3. _____

   _____

4. _____

   _____

5. _____

   _____

6. _____

   _____

7. _____

   _____

8. _____

   _____

9. _____

   _____

10. _____

    _____

Name: _____  Hector Suco  Date: _____

# Honesty Hour

"Honesty is the best policy," rings true especially for relationships. If you or your partner have issues and are holding them in, no matter how small, they can add a weight of stress in the relationship. Take one hour, every week or every month, to sit down with your partner and hash out all of the issues you have with them and them with you. Provide your partner with the same worksheet. You both will never agree on everything, but when it is out in the open, both partners will feel vindicated that their voice was heard. Practice this enough so that you will not need a worksheet and you will just be honest with each other all of the time!

1. List all of the issues that you have held in and not told your partner. If one issue is greatly important, use as many numbers as needed.

1. _____

2. _____

3. _____

4. _____

5. _____

6. _____

7. _____

8. _____

9. _____

10. _____

On the next page, you or your partner will write their response on the first line along with any and all possible solution(s) to each issue on the second line.

2. Either record your partner's response or have them respond to each issue. Use the second line provided to write any and all possible solutions to the issue.

1. _____

   _____

2. _____

   _____

3. _____

   _____

4. _____

   _____

5. _____

   _____

6. _____

   _____

7. _____

   _____

8. _____

   _____

9. _____

   _____

10. _____

    _____

Name: _____    Hector Suco    Date: _____

# Relationship Conflict Resolution

This worksheet is for one conflict within a relationship.

1. What is the conflict? Be specific.

   _____

   _____

2. How did it start?

   _____

3. Have you had this conflict before? Circle: Yes or No

4. How do you feel about this conflict?

   _____

   _____

5. How does your partner feel about this conflict?

   _____

   _____

6. How do/did you react to this conflict?

   _____

7. How can you react to this conflict in a more productive and effective way?

   _____

   _____

8. If your partner has the conflict with you, why do you think this is?

   _____

9. Do you think you can come to an agreement or compromise on this conflict? Why or why not?

_____

_____

_____

10. What do you see as the main issue? Circle:

You - Your Partner - The Problem - All

11. Do you both have a person you can trust to be fair, to be a mediator for this conflict/issue? If so, who?

_____

12. Write, in a productive and effective way, what you would like to tell your partner regarding a conflict you have not discussed yet, but want to.

_____

_____

_____

_____

_____

_____

_____

Name: _____    Hector Suco    Date: _____

# Relationship Conflict Resolution

This worksheet is for one conflict within a relationship.

1. What is the conflict? Be specific.

   _____

   _____

2. How did it start?

   _____

3. Have you had this conflict before? Circle: Yes or No

4. How do you feel about this conflict?

   _____

   _____

5. How does your partner feel about this conflict?

   _____

   _____

6. How do/did you react to this conflict?

   _____

7. How can you react to this conflict in a more productive and effective way?

   _____

   _____

8. If your partner has the conflict with you, why do you think this is?

   _____

9. Do you think you can come to an agreement or compromise on this conflict? Why or why not?

_____

_____

_____

10. What do you see as the main issue? Circle:

You - Your Partner - The Problem - All

11. Do you both have a person you can trust to be fair, to be a mediator for this conflict/issue? If so, who?

_____

12. Write, in a productive and effective way, what you would like to tell your partner regarding a conflict you have not discussed yet, but want to.

_____

_____

_____

_____

_____

_____

Name: _____    Hector Suco    Date: _____

# Relationship Conflict Resolution

This worksheet is for one conflict within a relationship.

1. What is the conflict? Be specific.

   _____

   _____

2. How did it start?

   _____

3. Have you had this conflict before? Circle: Yes or No

4. How do you feel about this conflict?

   _____

   _____

5. How does your partner feel about this conflict?

   _____

   _____

6. How do/did you react to this conflict?

   _____

7. How can you react to this conflict in a more productive and effective way?

   _____

   _____

8. If your partner has the conflict with you, why do you think this is?

   _____

9. Do you think you can come to an agreement or compromise on this conflict? Why or why not?

_____

_____

10. What do you see as the main issue? Circle:

You - Your Partner - The Problem - All

11. Do you both have a person you can trust to be fair, to be a mediator for this conflict/issue? If so, who?

_____

12. Write, in a productive and effective way, what you would like to tell your partner regarding a conflict you have not discussed yet, but want to.

_____

_____

_____

_____

_____

_____

Name: _____    Hector Suco    Date: _____

# Relationship Conflict Resolution

This worksheet is for one conflict within a relationship.

1. What is the conflict? Be specific.

   _____

   _____

2. How did it start?

   _____

3. Have you had this conflict before? Circle: Yes or No

4. How do you feel about this conflict?

   _____

   _____

5. How does your partner feel about this conflict?

   _____

   _____

6. How do/did you react to this conflict?

   _____

7. How can you react to this conflict in a more productive and effective way?

   _____

   _____

8. If your partner has the conflict with you, why do you think this is?

   _____

9. Do you think you can come to an agreement or compromise on this conflict? Why or why not?

_____

_____

_____

10. What do you see as the main issue? Circle:

You - Your Partner - The Problem - All

11. Do you both have a person you can trust to be fair, to be a mediator for this conflict/issue? If so, who?

_____

12. Write, in a productive and effective way, what you would like to tell your partner regarding a conflict you have not discussed yet, but want to.

_____

_____

_____

_____

_____

_____

Name: _____   Hector Suco   Date: _____

# Relationship Conflict Resolution

This worksheet is for one conflict within a relationship.

1. What is the conflict? Be specific.

   _____

   _____

2. How did it start?

   _____

3. Have you had this conflict before? Circle: Yes or No

4. How do you feel about this conflict?

   _____

   _____

5. How does your partner feel about this conflict?

   _____

   _____

6. How do/did you react to this conflict?

   _____

7. How can you react to this conflict in a more productive and effective way?

   _____

   _____

8. If your partner has the conflict with you, why do you think this is?

   _____

9. Do you think you can come to an agreement or compromise on this conflict? Why or why not?

_____

_____

_____

10. What do you see as the main issue? Circle:

You - Your Partner - The Problem - All

11. Do you both have a person you can trust to be fair, to be a mediator for this conflict/issue? If so, who?

_____

12. Write, in a productive and effective way, what you would like to tell your partner regarding a conflict you have not discussed yet, but want to.

_____

_____

_____

_____

_____

_____

_____

Name: _____    Hector Suco    Date: _____

# Relationship Conflict Resolution

This worksheet is for one conflict within a relationship.

1. What is the conflict? Be specific.

   _____

   _____

2. How did it start?

   _____

3. Have you had this conflict before? Circle: Yes or No

4. How do you feel about this conflict?

   _____

   _____

5. How does your partner feel about this conflict?

   _____

   _____

6. How do/did you react to this conflict?

   _____

7. How can you react to this conflict in a more productive and effective way?

   _____

   _____

8. If your partner has the conflict with you, why do you think this is?

   _____

9. Do you think you can come to an agreement or compromise on this conflict? Why or why not?

_____

_____

_____

10. What do you see as the main issue? Circle:

You - Your Partner - The Problem - All

11. Do you both have a person you can trust to be fair, to be a mediator for this conflict/issue? If so, who?

_____

12. Write, in a productive and effective way, what you would like to tell your partner regarding a conflict you have not discussed yet, but want to.

_____

_____

_____

_____

_____

_____

# Relationship Conflict Resolution Worksheet Guide

1. Explicitly write the problem down. Try not to include your emotions and convictions here. Also try not to place blame. Use "I" statements, like, "I feel XYZ when ABC happens."

2. Is one partner to blame or is this an issue both of you have contributed to? Look at the problem from the outside. Even if it is a fundamental disagreement, write down how it started.

3. Yes: This means that the problem has never been fully solved or compromises have not been made. It will continue throughout your relationship/marriage if it is not fully solved. It may be a deal breaker.

4. What are your emotions? Convictions? Do you feel you are right? Do you feel you have been wronged? Do you feel unappreciated? Do you feel like your opinions do not matter? Do you have negative emotions towards your partner with this conflict? Does your partner's attitude seem negative with this conflict?

5. How does your partner feel about this conflict? What are their emotions? Convictions? Do they feel they are right? Do they feel they have been wronged? Do they feel unappreciated? Do they feel like their opinions do not matter? Do they have negative emotions towards you with this conflict?

6. If this conflict is ongoing, how have you been reacting to it thus far? Have you confronted your partner? Do you believe you have handled this conflict in a productive and effective way? Have you stayed quiet and let it go by the wayside?

7. If you did respond in a negative manner, how can do you think you can react to this conflict in a more productive and effective way? It is never too late. Consider your partner's point of view. Look at all the possible solutions. Listen to what your partner is saying. You can ask a mediator to help you with this situation. You can compromise.

8. Does it have something to do with a past relationship or experience? If you do not know, ask them.

9. How can you compromise? What would it ultimately take for you to say that the conflict is resolved? An apology? An adjustment in behavior? Both you and your partner need to find peace at the end of this, consider what they want as well.

10. If you circled "You," the best thing is you now have the wherewithal to confront this issue and become a better person, not just for your partner, but also for yourself and everyone you love. You can do this. You should also be commended; it takes a lot of courage to admit that you are the source of the problem.

If you circled "Your partner," then your conflict is with them. You cannot change your partner. If that was your goal in the beginning, you have set yourself up for failure. Your best bet, if you think your partner is the root of this conflict, is to try and have them see things from your perspective. Tell them how you feel and how what is happening is affecting you.

If you circled, "The Problem," then you can definitely focus on the issue, see both sides, and come to an agreement with your partner.

If you've circled both, focus on one thing at a time.

11. A mediator is "a person who attempts to make people involved in a conflict come to an agreement; a go-between." This person can either be close to the situation or not. The best mediators are not biased. Some people believe problems should be kept between the people it involves - "do not wash your dirty laundry out in the streets." If you/your partner feel this way, you are going to have to solve this conflict on your own. Just remember that if no one is perfect and no relationship is perfect. This conflict will get worse if it is not solved. If you and your partner decide to use a mediator, but do not agree with their opinion, you may ask for a second opinion. If you also disagree with the second opinion, take some time to reflect on why you disagree and how your partner feels.

12. As you start writing your response, it is important to first mention what the problem is in a clear, unbiased way. Second, mention what you understand of how the other person feels about the conflict. Third, mention how you feel about the conflict, the possible solutions, your compromise, and your wish to resolve this conflict in order to move forward.

I hope this has helped you.
Good luck on your journey.

Name: _____  Hector Suco  Date: _____

# Romantic Attraction – When It Is Not Okay

This worksheet is to be filled out by someone who is in a relationship and may be attracted to someone else.

1. Are you still in love with your partner?

☐ Yes
☐ No
☐ I do not know

Explain your answer:

_____

_____

2. How happy are you with your partner?

0 —————————— 5 —————————— 10

3. If you were to guess, how happy is your partner with you?

0 —————————— 5 —————————— 10

4. Have you taken any action in regards to your feelings for this person?

☐ Yes and it will happen again
☐ Yes, but never again
☐ No, but I want to
☐ No, but I do not know if I want to
☐ Never have, never will

Explain your answer:

_____

_____

5. How long have you had these feelings? _____

6. Is your partner aware of these feelings? _____

7. Are you trying to pick between your partner and your crush?

☐ Yes (Continue below)
☐ No (Stop here)

| Partner: | | Person you are attracted to: | |
|---|---|---|---|
| Positive Attributes: | Negative Attributes: | Positive Attributes: | Negative Attributes: |
| | | | |
| | | | |
| | | | |
| | | | |
| | | | |

Describe how life will be like **with each** in the future…

Name: _____  Hector Suco  Date: _____

# Romantic Attraction – When It Is Not Okay

This worksheet is to be filled out by someone who is in a relationship and may be attracted to someone else.

1. Are you still in love with your partner?

☐ Yes
☐ No
☐ I do not know

Explain your answer:

_____

_____

2. How happy are you with your partner?

◄―――――――――――――+―――――――――――――►
0                            5                            10

3. If you were to guess, how happy is your partner with you?

◄―――――――――――――+―――――――――――――►
0                            5                            10

4. Have you taken any action in regards to your feelings for this person?

☐ Yes and it will happen again
☐ Yes, but never again
☐ No, but I want to
☐ No, but I do not know if I want to
☐ Never have, never will

Explain your answer:

_____

_____

5. How long have you had these feelings? _____

6. Is your partner aware of these feelings? _____

7. Are you trying to pick between your partner and your crush?

☐ Yes (Continue below)
☐ No (Stop here)

| Partner: || Person you are attracted to: ||
|---|---|---|---|
| Positive Attributes: | Negative Attributes: | Positive Attributes: | Negative Attributes: |
|  |  |  |  |
|  |  |  |  |
|  |  |  |  |
|  |  |  |  |
|  |  |  |  |

Describe how life will be like **with each** in the future…

Name: _____  Hector Suco  Date: _____

# Romantic Attraction — When It Is Not Okay

This worksheet is to be filled out by someone who is in a relationship and may be attracted to someone else.

1. Are you still in love with your partner?

☐ Yes
☐ No
☐ I do not know

Explain your answer:

_____

_____

2. How happy are you with your partner?

0 — 5 — 10

3. If you were to guess, how happy is your partner with you?

0 — 5 — 10

4. Have you taken any action in regards to your feelings for this person?

☐ Yes and it will happen again
☐ Yes, but never again
☐ No, but I want to
☐ No, but I do not know if I want to
☐ Never have, never will

Explain your answer:

_____

_____

5. How long have you had these feelings? _____

6. Is your partner aware of these feelings? _____

7. Are you trying to pick between your partner and your crush?

- ☐ Yes (Continue below)
- ☐ No (Stop here)

| Partner: | | Person you are attracted to: | |
|---|---|---|---|
| Positive Attributes: | Negative Attributes: | Positive Attributes: | Negative Attributes: |
|  |  |  |  |
|  |  |  |  |
|  |  |  |  |
|  |  |  |  |
|  |  |  |  |
| Describe how life will be like **with each** in the future… | | | |
|  | | | |

# Romantic Attraction – When It is Not Okay Worksheet Guide

1. If you are in a relationship and are attracted to someone else, the first thing you need to take a look is your relationship. Are you still in love with your partner? Use the *explain your answer* section to help you write your feelings down if you need to.

2. Continue your self-reflection by rating how happy you are with your partner currently. If there is a constant conflict with your partner, use the Relationship Conflict Resolution Worksheet if necessary.

3. Guess or ask them.

4. If you have taken action with the person you are attracted to, use the Romantic Betrayer Worksheet to take you through another set of questions you should reflect on.

If you have not taken any action, but want to take action, I urge you to reconsider.

If you do not know if you want to take action with the person you are attracted to, write down what you are feeling. What actions are you thinking about taking and what will the consequences of those actions be if you get caught? Are you willing to face those consequences? Are you willing to face your partner?

If you never have and never will, I applaud you. Use this worksheet to make sure you are aware of your feelings.

5. The length of time you have had feelings for this person matters. There is a line between attraction and obsession. There is a line between faithful and unfaithful. Try not to find yourself looking at their social media profiles on a daily basis or communicating with them arbitrarily. Work on your relationship. Decide what it is you ultimately want to do.

6. The answer to this question is based on how your interactions are with your partner. If your partner asks you questions, looks through your phone, become distant or less intimate, then they might be aware that something is going on. However, just because their behavior has not changed does not mean they are not aware. Other partners that may know how you feel may not show that they know.

7. You need to decide if your attraction to this person is worthwhile. The grass will not always be greener on the other side. Write down the positive and negative attributes of your partner and your crush, and then write what the future looks like with each of them. This can help you better understand your feelings and what you should do about them.

I hope this has helped you.
Good luck on your journey.

Name: _____     Hector Suco     Date: _____

# Romantic Betrayed

This worksheet is not a substitute for counseling. Please see a couples/marriage counselor at your earliest convenience.

1. What is/was your relationship status?
- ☐ Friends with Benefits (Go to #1A)
- ☐ Dating (Go to #1A)
- ☐ In A Relationship
- ☐ Engaged ☐
- ☐ Married
- ☐ Other: _____

1A. Is/Was this relationship exclusive?     ☐ Yes     ☐ No

2. Do you have any children with this person?

☐ Yes (Go to #2A)          ☐ No (Go to #3)

2A. How many? _____ 2B. How old are they? _____

2C. Do they know about the situation? _____

3. Are you still with this person currently?

☐ Yes     ☐ No     ☐ Separated     ☐ On/Off     ☐ We haven't spoken

☐ I do not know

4. List the people who know about the situation.

_____   _____   _____   _____

_____   _____   _____   _____

5. Is this the first occurrence?     ☐ Yes     ☐ No (5A)

5A. How many times has this happened before? _____

6. How long has this betrayal been going on? _____

7. How many people are involved in this situation? _____

8. Is this a suspicion you have or do you have proof?

☐ Suspicion (Go to #8A - B)   ☐ Confirmed (Go to #8C - D)

8A. What behaviors or behavior changes do you find suspicious? _____

_____

8B. Would you consider yourself a suspicious person? _____

_____

8C. What is the hard evidence for this betrayal? _____

_____

8D. Has there been a confession? _____

9. Is there any way of saving this relationship?
☐ Yes (Go to #9A - B)
☐ No (Go to #9C)

9A. How? What are the steps you (and your partner) will have to take to make amends?

1. _____

2. _____

3. _____

4. _____

5. _____

6. _____

7. _____

8. _____

9B. Have you forgiven your partner? If not, are you planning to? Explain.

_____

_____

9C. What will be the next step for the two of you?

☐ Stop seeing each other    ☐ Break Up    ☐ Call off the wedding

☐ Divorce    ☐ Separation    ☐ I do not know

10. How challenging would it be to trust them or someone else again?

_____

_____

11. Do you have any idea what caused this betrayal?

_____

_____

12. Did you learn any lessons from this betrayal?

_____

_____

13. As you would do in a journal/diary, use this space to list and explain any grievances you have about the situation:

_____

_____

_____

_____

_____

Name: _____    Hector Suco    Date: _____

# Romantic Betrayed

This worksheet is not a substitute for counseling. Please see a couples/marriage counselor at your earliest convenience.

1. What is/was your relationship status?
   ☐ Friends with Benefits (Go to #1A)
   ☐ Dating (Go to #1A)
   ☐ In A Relationship
   ☐ Engaged ☐
   ☐ Married
   ☐ Other: _____

1A. Is/Was this relationship exclusive?    ☐ Yes    ☐ No

2. Do you have any children with this person?

☐ Yes (Go to #2A)        ☐ No (Go to #3)

2A. How many? _____ 2B. How old are they? _____

2C. Do they know about the situation? _____

3. Are you still with this person currently?

☐ Yes    ☐ No    ☐ Separated    ☐ On/Off    ☐ We haven't spoken

☐ I do not know

4. List the people who know about the situation.

_____  _____  _____  _____

_____  _____  _____  _____

5. Is this the first occurrence?    ☐ Yes    ☐ No (5A)

5A. How many times has this happened before? _____

6. How long has this betrayal been going on? _____

7. How many people are involved in this situation? _____

8. Is this a suspicion you have or do you have proof?

☐  Suspicion (Go to #8A - B)   ☐  Confirmed (Go to #8C - D)

8A. What behaviors or behavior changes do you find suspicious? _____
_____

8B. Would you consider yourself a suspicious person? _____
_____

8C. What is the hard evidence for this betrayal? _____
_____

8D. Has there been a confession? _____

9. Is there any way of saving this relationship?
☐  Yes (Go to #9A - B)
☐  No (Go to #9C)

9A. How? What are the steps you (and your partner) will have to take to make amends?

1. _____

2. _____

3. _____

4. _____

5. _____

6. _____

7. _____

8. _____

9B. Have you forgiven your partner? If not, are you planning to? Explain.

_____

_____

9C. What will be the next step for the two of you?

☐ Stop seeing each other ☐ Break Up ☐ Call off the wedding

☐ Divorce ☐ Separation ☐ I do not know

10. How challenging would it be to trust them or someone else again?

_____

_____

11. Do you have any idea what caused this betrayal?

_____

_____

12. Did you learn any lessons from this betrayal?

_____

_____

13. As you would do in a journal/diary, use this space to list and explain any grievances you have about the situation:

_____

_____

_____

_____

# Romantic Betrayed Worksheet Guide

1A. The term *exclusive* is important here. That's why friends with benefits and dating fall into the next question. If your relationship with your partner is not formalized, then it may be unclear whether or not it is okay to talk to or date others. Exclusive relationships such as being a couple, engaged, or married has a much more serious tone.

2. Having children does not define a relationship, but it does have an effect on the situation as far as them knowing and potentially helping you through the process. If you and your partner are amicable, staying together for your children is not a bad idea. However, depending on your values, spiritual feelings, and level of conflict should determine whether or not you would want to stay together. If your relationship with your partner becomes toxic, you may want to consider separating.

3. If you picked I don't know, find out.

4. Some people believe that family business should stay in the family. Others believe in being able to vent and talk things out. Do what helps you heal.

5. "Once a cheater always a cheater" is quite a common thought, and there is such a thing as a serial cheater. If your partner has cheated more than once, and especially if they have cheated in past relationships, they may have a problem.

8. A betrayal can be anything from going on an innocent lunch date with a coworker to having an affair.

8A. Suspicious behavior can include a change in tone of voice, habits, interests, etc. Other suspicious behaviors could include, but are not limited to: emotional responses to certain questions, arriving home a different way than they left, leaving or arriving to work/home late, etc.

8B. People who are suspicious usually have their own reasons for being that way, their trust has usually been broken. That should be respected, but it should not bias judgment.

8C. Evidence may include notes from someone, a hotel business card, an unknown phone number, deleted phone calls, text messages with someone, deleted text messages, etc.

8D. Did they confess out of guilt or out of a desire to admit their mistake and move past it with you? After a confession, seek help from family, friends, and a counselor if and when it happens.

9. Really think on this. Think how staying together or breaking up will affect you.

9A. In no particular order, the possible steps include, but are not limited to, receiving an apology, working on communication skills, reigniting romance, clear expectations moving forward, attending a couple's retreat, couples counselor, etc.

9B. "To err is human. To forgive: divine"
—Alexander Pope.

Even if you do not formally accept the forgiveness, it should be given to you either way. You deserve it.

10. Trust takes years to build and seconds to destroy. Trust needs to be earned, so when it is broken, it may be difficult to trust anyone again. Some people are turned off completely after a betrayal. Love should not die because of a betrayal. There are honest people out there. Do not believe everyone will betray you.

11. According to researchers from the University of Tennessee, there are several reasons why people cheat.
-Avoiding intimacy for fear of getting hurt
-More intimacy needed; No communication
-Newness/Libido boost
-Control & Power
-Lack of willpower
-Variety
-Not caught yet

12. People can learn many lessons from a romantic betrayal. Some will find the courage to leave, while others may use the event to strengthen their relationship. Many will be more cautious after this and others still may be driven to be more honest with their partner.

13. Try not to share your intimate secrets with those whom you do not trust. The way you feel now may be different than how you feel this time next year. Come back to this worksheet to see how you viewed yourself and your situation at this point in your life, then compare and contrast. How have things changed?

I hope this has helped you.
Good luck on your journey.

Name: _____  Hector Suco  Date: _____

# Romantic Betrayer

This worksheet is for anyone who has betrayed or believes they have betrayed their partner. It is for those who have accepted what they have done and feel remorse and/or guilt for their actions.

1. What is/was your relationship status?
   - ☐ Friends with Benefits (Go to #1A)
   - ☐ Dating (Go to #1A)
   - ☐ In A Relationship
   - ☐ Engaged ☐
   - ☐ Married
   - ☐ Other: _____

1A. Was this relationship exclusive?    ☐ Yes    ☐ No

2. Are you still in a relationship with this person?
   ☐ Yes    ☐ No    ☐ Separate    ☐ On/Off    ☐ We haven't spoken

   ☐ I do not know

3. Was this the first occurrence?    ☐ Yes    ☐ No (Go to #3A)

3A. How many times has this happened before? _____

4. Have you stopped?

   ☐ Yes            ☐ No

5. Does your partner know?    ☐ Yes    ☐ No (5A)

5A. Are you planning on saying something?
   ☐ Yes (Go to #5B)
   ☐ No (Go to #5C – 5E)

5B. When? What is your plan? _____
_____

5C. How much longer will it be until they know? _____

5D. How do you see this ending? _____

5E. Do you think you will continue to hurt the person you are betraying? Explain.

_____

_____

6. Are you trying to choose between your partner and the person you cheated with?
   ☐   Yes (Go to #6A)
   ☐   No (Go to #7)

6A.

Partner: _____    Person You Cheated With: _____

| Positive Attributes: | Negative Attributes: | Positive Attributes: | Negative Attributes |
|---|---|---|---|
|  |  |  |  |
|  |  |  |  |
|  |  |  |  |
|  |  |  |  |
|  |  |  |  |

Describe how life will be like **with each** in the future…

_____   _____

_____   _____

_____   _____

_____   _____

_____   _____

_____   _____

_____   _____

_____   _____

7. Why did you do what you did? Look into your past or current relationships for an answer. Was there something missing? A break in communication? A lack of intimacy? Explain.

_____

_____

_____

_____

_____

8. Do you and your partner want to stay in this relationship?

☐ Yes (Continue)   ☐ No (Go to #12)

9. What are some ways you can build/earn trust with your partner?

_____

_____

10. How long do you think it will take for them to trust you again?

_____

_____

11. What does the phrase "trust takes years to build, seconds to break, and forever to repair" mean to you?

_____

_____

_____

_____

12. Have you asked your partner for forgiveness?

- ☐ Yes: What did they say? _____
- ☐ No (Go to #12A)

12A. Do you plan to ask them for forgiveness?

- ☐ Yes: When? _____
- ☐ No: Why not? _____

13. Have you forgiven yourself for the actions you have taken? Explain.

_____

_____

14. What lessons did you learn from this?

_____

_____

_____

_____

_____

_____

_____

Name: _____  Hector Suco  Date: _____

# Romantic Betrayer

This worksheet is for anyone who has betrayed or believes they have betrayed their partner. It is for those who have accepted what they have done and feel remorse and/or guilt for their actions.

1. What is/was your relationship status?
   - ☐ Friends with Benefits (Go to #1A)
   - ☐ Dating (Go to #1A)
   - ☐ In A Relationship
   - ☐ Engaged ☐
   - ☐ Married
   - ☐ Other: _____

1A. Was this relationship exclusive?   ☐ Yes   ☐ No

2. Are you still in a relationship with this person?
   ☐ Yes   ☐ No   ☐ Separate   ☐ On/Off   ☐ We haven't spoken

   ☐ I do not know

3. Was this the first occurrence?   ☐ Yes     ☐ No (Go to #3A)

3A. How many times has this happened before? _____

4. Have you stopped?

   ☐ Yes                              ☐ No

5. Does your partner know?   ☐ Yes     ☐ No (5A)

5A. Are you planning on saying something?
   ☐ Yes (Go to #5B)
   ☐ No (Go to #5C – 5E)

5B. When? What is your plan? _____
_____

5C. How much longer will it be until they know? _____

5D. How do you see this ending? _____

5E. Do you think you will continue to hurt the person you are betraying? Explain.

_____

_____

6. Are you trying to choose between your partner and the person you cheated with?
- ☐ Yes (Go to #6A)
- ☐ No (Go to #7)

6A.

Partner: _____ | Person You Cheated With: _____

| Positive Attributes: | Negative Attributes: | Positive Attributes: | Negative Attributes |
|---|---|---|---|
|  |  |  |  |
|  |  |  |  |
|  |  |  |  |
|  |  |  |  |
|  |  |  |  |

Describe how life will be like **with each** in the future…

_____  _____

_____  _____

_____  _____

_____  _____

_____  _____

_____  _____

_____  _____

7. Why did you do what you did? Look into your past or current relationships for an answer. Was there something missing? A break in communication? A lack of intimacy? Explain.

_____

_____

_____

_____

_____

8. Do you and your partner want to stay in this relationship?

☐ Yes (Continue)     ☐ No (Go to #12)

9. What are some ways you can build/earn trust with your partner?

_____

_____

10. How long do you think it will take for them to trust you again?

_____

_____

11. What does the phrase "trust takes years to build, seconds to break, and forever to repair" mean to you?

_____

_____

_____

_____

12. Have you asked your partner for forgiveness?

☐ Yes: What did they say? _____

☐ No (Go to #12A)

12A. Do you plan to ask them for forgiveness?

☐ Yes: When? _____

☐ No: Why not? _____

13. Have you forgiven yourself for the actions you have taken? Explain.

_____

_____

14. What lessons did you learn from this?

_____

_____

_____

_____

_____

_____

_____

# Romantic Betrayer Worksheet Guide

1A. The term *exclusive* is important here. If you and your partner's relationship was not formalized, than it is considered okay to talk to or date others. Exclusive relationships such as being a couple, engaged, or married takes on a much more serious tone. If your lover still has issues with this, make it clear that you two were not exclusive. The lesson learned here is that "exclusive" needs to be explicitly stated in all circumstances of a relationship.

2. Words matter. Be clear with your partner about the situation. Ask for clarity if you are uncertain.

3. If you are or think you may be a serial cheater, consider getting professional help.

4. If this is still going on, remember that this worksheet is for those who have accepted what they have done and feel remorse and/or guilty for their actions. Consider why the betrayal is going on.

5C. The truth will come out sooner or later. Exercise caution. Come clean and unburden yourself.

5D. What is your ultimate motivation? What are you gaining? What do you need to prove?

5E. To answer this question, practice empathy. Put yourself in the shoes of the person you are betraying.

6. Trying to choose between two people is often difficult. Write down the positive and negative attributes of your partner and the person you cheated with. Then, write what you think the future will look like with each of them. This can help you make a more informed decision.

7. According to researchers from the University of Tennessee, psychologists have pointed to several reasons why people cheat.
-Avoiding intimacy for fear of getting hurt
-More intimacy needed; No communication
-Newness/Libido boost
-Control & Power
-Lack of willpower
-Variety
-Not caught yet

8. If you picked no, make sure it is a hard no. Ask for clarity, unless it is obvious.

9. There are many ways you can build and earn the trust of others. Examples include:

| Reliable | Honesty | Open | Ethics | Show Integrity |
|---|---|---|---|---|
| Keep my word | Tell the truth | Say more than needed | Have strong morals | Be more loyal |
| Do not cancel | If I lie, I will own up to it | Show others I care | Show fairness | Show more awareness |
| Keep promises; Create a stronger bond | Do not omit important things | Openly about my feelings | Stay neutral during difficult times | Stay away from double standards |

10. & 11. The phrase "trust takes years to build, seconds to break, and forever to repair" speaks volumes. As one of the foundations of any relationship (romantic, familial, friendship, etc.), trust is like the roots of a tree. Imagine trust, communication, and honesty as the roots of a tree representing a simple relationship. A break in trust means that there was also a break in honesty and communication. This causes the whole tree to fall. That's why, like a tree, relationships would "take years to build and grow, seconds to break and fall, and forever to repair."

12. "To err is human. To forgive: divine"
–Alexander Pope.

If you have admitted what you have done to your partner, asking their forgiveness may give you a good idea as to how they are feeling and where your relationship might be heading.

13. As you ask for the forgiveness of others for what you have done, do not forget to forgive yourself once you have deeply thought on your actions.

14. What were the lessons learned? People can learn many lessons from a romantic betrayal. Some find out they had a lot of courage to get through this episode. Some find there is a light at the end of the tunnel. Some might even say a romantic betrayal may have made their relationship stronger.

Good luck on your journey.
I hope this has helped you.

Name: _____     Hector Suco     Date: _____

# Marriage Separation

This worksheet is for married couples that are separated. If separation is an option, but not official, try the Marriage Worksheet or Relationship Conflict Resolution Worksheet.

1. There are many degrees of separation. Below are my options and their definitions. How would you describe your current situation?

|   | Status | Definition | Answer Questions |
|---|--------|------------|------------------|
| ☐ | On A Break | Separated and not exclusive: Can date/see other people. Chance of reconciling is there. | All |
| ☐ | Not Talking | No communication, unless it is a must. Possibly in the process of divorce. | Skip to #9 |
| ☐ | Friends With Benefits | Not together. Sexual relationship with no feelings. | All. Also, use my Friends With Benefits Worksheet |

2. What is/are the issue(s) in your marriage? How can it be fixed? What will it take to start rebuilding your marriage?

_____

_____

_____

3. Have you ever been to see a marriage counselor?

☐ Yes: How often have you gone?

_____

☐ No: Would you ever go see a marriage counselor? Why or why not?

_____

4. Have you or your partner gone on dates with other people? Have you told each other?

___

5. Have rules and boundaries been set for this "break"? If so, what are they?

___

___

6. Is there a time limit to this break? If so, what is it? If not, what do you think it should be?

___

7. When you spend time with your spouse, is it just the two of you or do you spend time with other people?

___

8. Is there a chance your marriage can be reconciled? Explain.

___

9. Has there ever been a booty call between the two of you?

___

10. Who initiated the separation?

☐ Myself  ☐ My partner (Skip #11)  ☐ Mutual

11. Do you regret your decision?  ☐ Yes  ☐ No (Go to #15)

12. Do you want to try and reconcile with your partner so you can fix your marriage together?
- ☐ Yes (Go to #13; Skip #14)
- ☐ Yes, but (I think) they are seeing someone else (Go to #15)
- ☐ I do not know (Skip #13)
- ☐ No (Go to #15)

13. Have you told them how you feel?

- ☐ Yes: What did they say?

_____

- ☐ No: Why not?

| 14. Below, list your partner's positive and negative attributes. Then, describe what you think life will be like in the future with and without them in your life. ||
|---|---|
| Positive Attributes: | Negative Attributes: |
|  |  |
|  |  |
|  |  |
|  |  |
|  |  |
| Describe how life will be like in the future… ||
| …with them. | …without them. |
|  |  |
|  |  |
|  |  |
|  |  |
|  |  |

15. How do you feel about the separation?

- ☐ Ecstatic (Go to #21)
- ☐ Happy (Go to #21)
- ☐ I do not know (Go to #16)
- ☐ Sad (Go to #16)
- ☐ Depressed (Go to #16)

16. Where are you in the 5 Stages of Loss?

- ☐ Denial ☐ Anger ☐ Bargaining ☐ Depression
- ☐ Acceptance

17. How much time have you spent thinking about this separation?

_____

18. Write down some of the thoughts you have about the separation.

_____

_____

_____

_____

19. Do you believe that a higher power that is helping and guiding you?

_____

20. Do you believe there is a divine plan that is set for you?

_____

21. What are some things you have learned from this experience? How are you not going to let it happen again?

_____

_____

_____

Name: _____     Hector Suco     Date: _____

# Marriage Separation

This worksheet is for married couples that are separated. If separation is an option, but not official, try my Marriage Worksheet or Relationship Conflict Resolution Worksheet.

1. There are many degrees of separation. Below are my options and their definitions. How would you describe your current situation?

|   | Status | Definition | Answer Questions |
|---|---|---|---|
| ☐ | On A Break | Separated and not exclusive: Can date/see other people. Chance of reconciling is there. | All |
| ☐ | Not Talking | No communication, unless it is a must. Possibly in the process of divorce. | Skip to #9 |
| ☐ | Friends With Benefits | Not together. Sexual relationship with no feelings. | All. Also, use my Friends With Benefits Worksheet |

2. What is/are the issue(s) in your marriage? How can it be fixed? What will it take to start rebuilding your marriage?

_____

_____

_____

3. Have you ever been to see a marriage counselor?

☐  Yes: How often have you gone?

_____

☐  No: Would you ever go see a marriage counselor? Why or why not?

_____

4. Have you or your partner gone on dates with other people? Have you told each other?

_____

5. Have rules and boundaries been set for this "break"? If so, what are they?

_____

_____

6. Is there a time limit to this break? If so, what is it? If not, what do you think it should be?

_____

7. When you spend time with your spouse, is it just the two of you or do you spend time with other people?

_____

8. Is there a chance your marriage can be reconciled? Explain.

_____

9. Has there ever been a booty call between the two of you?

_____

10. Who initiated the separation?

☐ Myself  ☐ My partner (Skip #11)  ☐ Mutual

11. Do you regret your decision?  ☐ Yes  ☐ No (Go to #15)

12. Do you want to try and reconcile with your partner so you can fix your marriage together?
- ☐ Yes (Go to #13; Skip #14)
- ☐ Yes, but (I think) they are seeing someone else (Go to #15)
- ☐ I do not know (Skip #13)
- ☐ No (Go to #15)

13. Have you told them how you feel?

☐ Yes: What did they say?

_____

☐ No: Why not?

| 14. Below, list your partner's positive and negative attributes. Then, describe what you think life will be like in the future with and without them in your life. ||
|---|---|
| Positive Attributes: | Negative Attributes: |
|  |  |
|  |  |
|  |  |
|  |  |
|  |  |
| Describe how life will be like in the future… ||
| …with them. | …without them. |
|  |  |
|  |  |
|  |  |
|  |  |
|  |  |

15. How do you feel about the separation?

- ☐ Ecstatic (Go to #21)
- ☐ Happy (Go to #21)
- ☐ I do not know (Go to #16)
- ☐ Sad (Go to #16)
- ☐ Depressed (Go to #16)

16. Where are you in the 5 Stages of Loss?

☐ Denial    ☐ Anger    ☐ Bargaining    ☐ Depression

☐ Acceptance

17. How much time have you spent thinking about this separation?

_____

18. Write down some of the thoughts you have about the separation.

_____

_____

_____

_____

19. Do you believe that a higher power that is helping and guiding you?

_____

20. Do you believe there is a divine plan that is set for you?

_____

21. What are some things you have learned from this experience? How are you not going to let it happen again?

_____

_____

_____

# Marriage Separation Worksheet Guide

1. Everyone has different ideas of what a separation means and not every separation is the same. These particular separation scenarios are broad and made to cover everyone across the spectrum. With each status, I guide the user to which question they should go next and whether they should skip or stop at a question.

2. Disagreements will always happen in relationships and marriages. Some of these disputes can last minutes, while others can last for weeks. Spouses would usually call it quits if these disagreements do not seem to get resolved over a period of time. The cause of this is usually a violation of one's values and/or deal breakers. An angry outburst can also cause the receiver to fear their partner. Although the causes of fights will be too long to list here, what is/are the main cause of your disagreement(s)? How can it be fixed (compromises)? Decide what needs to be done to get this marriage back on track.

3. Marriage counselors have studied the issues of intimacy. They have a vast reservoir of experiences and advice for any couple. My wife and I have gone to a marriage counselor without having anything really "wrong". Sometimes is a good idea to just get an opinion from an (educated) outsider. You do not necessarily need to see a counselor, but a yearly talk about where you've been, what problems you are having and how to solve them is very healthy for all marriages.

4. - 6. If you've ever seen the TV show, *Friends*, then you know all about Rachel and Ross and their relationship rollercoaster. Rachel wanted "a break" from her relationship with Ross. The expectations of the break were never discussed. Ross thought that she meant that she wanted to end the relationship, while Rachel meant that she wanted them to spend some time apart without ending their relationship. Ross sleeps with another woman and gets caught by Rachel. Rachel sees this as a betrayal, while Ross justifies it by saying "we were on a break." That concept continues to come up throughout the series, but also demonstrates the potential problems when two people "take a break" from each other. If you want to or are on a break right now, set boundaries, set a time limit, and be honest with each other about what you want/expect each other to do or not do during the break.

7 - 8. When separated, one of two things can happen; either you stay married or separate (and possibly divorce). A marriage separation is a period of time that can be considered the purgatory stage, a place somewhere in the middle that has no clear direction and can last for an indefinite amount of time. If there is a possibility of getting back together, do not stay separated for a long time. The longer you are separated, the harder it will be to get together and talk things out.

9. According to the most accepted definition on Urban Dictionary, a booty call is "A late night summons -- often made via telephone -- to arrange clandestine sexual liaisons on an ad hoc basis." A booty call has no place in a marriage or a separation unless it is being used as a tool to reignite the romance.
Source: www.urbandictionary.com

13. If you have told your still-current spouse about wanting to get back together, their response should tell you a lot. A "yes" answer paves the road for a reunion. A "maybe" or "I need time to think about it" signifies that there needs to be time and work put in to make sure that the issues are dealt with. A "No" is unfortunate. Try to talk things out, but be respectful of their final decision.

14. If you do not know if you want to get back together, write down your partner's positive and negative attributes so that you can compare. Also write what you think life will be like with and without them. Use this to help you with your decision.

15. I do say that if you feel ecstatic or happy, to go to #21, but you can go to #16 if you wish.

16. Self-talk, termed by Albert Ellis, refers to the running commentary that goes on in your mind during the day. Below are examples of self-talk in each stage of loss:

| Denial | "We are not really broken up." "They're just kidding." "They're all talk." "We are still together." "They're going to want me back." |
|---|---|
| Anger | "What did I do wrong?" "How stupid can I be?" "It is their fault." |
| Bargaining | "What if I change?" "What can I do to get them back?" "Can I write them a love letter?" |
| Depression | "I suck at being a partner." "It was never meant to be." "I'll never find true love." "Why is this happening to me?" |
| Acceptance | "I will be okay." "I will find true love again." "It is better this way." "I've learned a lot from this experience." |

17. You should not obsess about this separation. If you are thinking about it every ten minutes, your productivity at work may falter, your family may dislike it, and you may doubt your own self worth.

18. As stated in #16, self-talk is the running commentary that goes on in your mind during the day. Most of it means very little, but it can become a problem when your thinking turns into harmful beliefs about yourself and/or your ex. Many studies have found a link between irrational beliefs and anxiety. Look for reasons (even little ones) to be satisfied and happy with your life, no matter what you are going through. Always try to find the silver lining.

"Psychologist Ethan Kross found that how people conduct their inner monologues has an enormous effect on their success in life. Talk to yourself with the pronoun *I*, for instance, and you're likely to fluster and perform poorly in stressful circumstances. Address yourself by your name and your chances of acing a host of tasks, from speech making to self-advocacy, suddenly soar."
-Pamela Weintraub "The Voice of Reason"
*Psychology Today*
May 4th, 2015

19 - 20. Turn to religion if you need extra guidance in your life. Remember your vows and see what can work for you.

21. Whether or not you decide to stay with your spouse, you still need to learn from this experience. What are some of the things that you have learned? How are you going to make sure that something like this does not happen again? If you do decide to get a divorce and remarry, how are you going to make sure the same thing doesn't happen with your new spouse?

I hope this has helped you.
Good luck on your journey.

Name: _____  Hector Suco  Date: _____

# Divorce

This worksheet is for anyone who is divorced or is in the process of getting divorced.

1. What is your status?
☐ Separated
☐ In the process of getting divorced
☐ Divorced

2. Who pushed for this divorce?
☐ Myself
☐ My spouse (Go to #2A)
☐ Mutual

2A. Did you agree to it or would you give reconciliation a chance?

_____

3. How long have you been married for? _____

4. Is this your first divorce?
☐ Yes
☐ No: How many times have you been divorced? _____

5. What was the best part of your marriage?*

_____

_____

6. What was the worst part of your marriage?*

_____

_____

*At this point in the worksheet, stop and compare your answers for numbers five and six. Do they seem balanced to you? Does one answer outweigh the other?

_____

_____

7. How long did it take for you to decide that you could no longer be with your spouse?
- ☐ Years
- ☐ Months
- ☐ A few weeks
- ☐ A few days
- ☐ In an instant
- ☐ I still want to be with my spouse

8. What was the first issue you had with your spouse?

_____

_____

8A. What was the second issue you had with your spouse?

_____

_____

8B. What was the third issue you had with your spouse?

_____

_____

9. Did you and your spouse go see a marriage counselor when things turned for the worst?

_____

_____

10. Was there a last straw? If so, what was it?

_____

_____

11. What would you say is/was the ultimate cause of your divorce?

_____

_____

12. Did you and your spouse have children?
- ☐ No (Go to #13)
- ☐ Yes (Go to #12A)

12A: How old are they?
_____

12B: How do/did they feel about the divorce?
_____
_____

13. Would you ever want to marry someone else in the future?
- ☐ No (Skip #14)
- ☐ Not sure yet (Skip #14)
- ☐ Yes (Go to #14)

14. How will it be different next time? How will **you** be different next time?
_____
_____
_____

15. What type of relationship do you plan to have with your ex?
_____
_____
_____

16. How have your feelings about marriage changed because of this divorce?
_____
_____
_____
_____

Name: _____    Hector Suco    Date: _____

# Divorce

This worksheet is for anyone who is divorced or is in the process of getting divorced.

1. What is your status?
☐ Separated
☐ In the process of getting divorced
☐ Divorced

2. Who pushed for this divorce?
☐ Myself
☐ My spouse (Go to #2A)
☐ Mutual

2A. Did you agree to it or would you give reconciliation a chance?

_____

3. How long have you been married for? _____

4. Is this your first divorce?
☐ Yes
☐ No: How many times have you been divorced? _____

5. What was the best part of your marriage?*

_____

_____

6. What was the worst part of your marriage?*

_____

_____

*At this point in the worksheet, stop and compare your answers for numbers five and six. Do they seem balanced to you? Does one answer outweigh the other?

_____

_____

7. How long did it take for you to decide that you could no longer be with your spouse?
- ☐ Years
- ☐ Months
- ☐ A few weeks
- ☐ A few days
- ☐ In an instant
- ☐ I still want to be with my spouse

8. What was the first issue you had with your spouse?

_____

_____

8A. What was the second issue you had with your spouse?

_____

_____

8B. What was the third issue you had with your spouse?

_____

_____

9. Did you and your spouse go see a marriage counselor when things turned for the worst?

_____

_____

10. Was there a last straw? If so, what was it?

_____

_____

11. What would you say is/was the ultimate cause of your divorce?

_____

_____

12. Did you and your spouse have children?
- ☐ No (Go to #13)
- ☐ Yes (Go to #12A)

12A: How old are they?
_____

12B: How do/did they feel about the divorce?
_____
_____

13. Would you ever want to marry someone else in the future?
- ☐ No (Skip #14)
- ☐ Not sure yet (Skip #14)
- ☐ Yes (Go to #14)

14. How will it be different next time? How will **you** be different next time?
_____
_____
_____

15. What type of relationship do you plan to have with your ex?
_____
_____
_____

16. How have your feelings about marriage changed because of this divorce?
_____
_____
_____

Name: _____  Hector Suco  Date: _____

# Divorce

This worksheet is for anyone who is divorced or is in the process of getting divorced.

1. What is your status?
☐ Separated
☐ In the process of getting divorced
☐ Divorced

2. Who pushed for this divorce?
☐ Myself
☐ My spouse (Go to #2A)
☐ Mutual

2A. Did you agree to it or would you give reconciliation a chance?
_____

3. How long have you been married for? _____

4. Is this your first divorce?
☐ Yes
☐ No: How many times have you been divorced? _____

5. What was the best part of your marriage?*
_____
_____

6. What was the worst part of your marriage?*
_____
_____

*At this point in the worksheet, stop and compare your answers for numbers five and six. Do they seem balanced to you? Does one answer outweigh the other?
_____
_____

7. How long did it take for you to decide that you could no longer be with your spouse?
- ☐ Years
- ☐ Months
- ☐ A few weeks
- ☐ A few days
- ☐ In an instant
- ☐ I still want to be with my spouse

8. What was the first issue you had with your spouse?

_____

_____

8A. What was the second issue you had with your spouse?

_____

_____

8B. What was the third issue you had with your spouse?

_____

_____

9. Did you and your spouse go see a marriage counselor when things turned for the worst?

_____

_____

10. Was there a last straw? If so, what was it?

_____

_____

11. What would you say is/was the ultimate cause of your divorce?

_____

_____

12. Did you and your spouse have children?
- ☐ No
- ☐ Yes:

How old are they? _____

How do/did they feel about the divorce? _____

_____

13. Would you ever want to marry someone else in the future?
- ☐ No (Skip #14)
- ☐ Not sure yet (Skip #14)
- ☐ Yes (Go to #14)

14. How will it be different next time? How will **you** be different next time?

_____

_____

_____

15. What type of relationship do you plan to have with you ex?

_____

_____

_____

16. How have your feelings about marriage changed because of this divorce?

_____

_____

_____

# Divorce Worksheet Guide

2. Divorce is usually initiated by one spouse or the other. Irreconcilable differences take a toll. The partner that thinks they have suffered the most is usually the one that suggests separating. If the decision to get a divorce is mutual, then the relationship may have been deteriorating for a period of time.

2A. Be clear about your feelings. Write down anything that you think can help you make a better decision about yourself and your life. If you agreed to the divorce because the feelings were mutual, that is fine. If you agreed to it because you didn't think there was a chance to save the marriage, then this might be a decision you regret for a very long time. If this is true, take a chance and tell your spouse/ex exactly how you feel. You have nothing to lose.

3. The length of your marriage may, more or less, determine how much time it will take you to get over this and eventually move on.

4. If this is not your first divorce, do you notice a pattern between your previous and current relationships?

5. Focus on the things that made you smile, laugh, blush, or fall even more in love with your spouse while you were together.

6. This could be the reason(s) for the divorce or something else entirely.

*If your answer for number five is more important than your answer to number six, I urge you to reconsider your decision to divorce. You may be making a big mistake. Look back at your marriage (use the other worksheets) and see if there is any possibility that you and your spouse can reconcile. If your answer for number six more impactful than your answer to number five, than this divorce may be the best thing for you both.

7. When people make big decisions, they should take time to think. Did your spouse take more time to think? Did you take more time?

8. Write out the issues that started the decline in your marriage. It is important that you describe them here to serve as a guide for you to understand and improve your next relationship. At the very least, you learned something you do not like and that can be just as good as learning something you do like. If these problems can be solved with some good old-fashioned hard work, then you might want to reconsider.

9. Marriage counselors have studied for years so that they can help couples just like you. They have a vast reservoir of experiences and knowledge to share, and probably some wisdom from their own lives. My wife and I have gone to a marriage counselor as a "marriage check up." We didn't have any pressing problems, but it helped us better understand our relationship. Decide together whether or not you both want to see a marriage. It would make a huge difference. I would suggest you go see one whether your divorce is finalized or not.

10. It is important to pinpoint the moments that defined your marriage, good or bad. If you and your spouse end up in court, you should be able to give an account of your marriage that is unbiased as possible.

11. The cause of a conflict is usually just below the surface. It deals with a conflict of values. "Your spouse never putting the dishes away" is not the true cause for divorce. "Not feeling valued as a person by your partner" or "having a partner betray your trust" are causes for divorce.

12. My parents got divorced when I was sixteen. It was tough. Make sure your children understand what is going on during this process, but emphasize peace and civility if possible. Try not to bad-mouth your spouse or undermine their parenting in front of your children.

13. Divorce doesn't have to be the end of your love life. Some people keep that the possibility of finding new love open, while others will say that they will never get married again. Decide what is best for you moving forward.

14. Do not just place blame on your past partner(s), look inside yourself and try to figure out what went wrong and why. Once you do that, you can learn from your mistakes.

15. You do not actually need to have a relationship with your ex after you divorce, especially if there are no responsibilities (i.e. children or combined financial interests) that tie you both together. Some couples choose to remain on good terms, especially for the sake of their children, but other couples are unable to maintain such civility. Figure out whether or not you are okay with seeing and/or spending time with your ex. You might even want to talk about it together. Marriage forms a bond that is not necessarily very easy to break off and forget. Sometimes comfort and familiarity are hard to give up.

16. Your views may not have changed at all. Some people will say that marriage is still a sacred bond that occurs when two people deeply love each other, even after their divorce. Others will say that two people are not always meant to be together forever. Write down how you use to feel about marriage before your divorce as well as how you currently feel. Then compare the two.

I hope this has helped you.
Good luck on your journey.

Name: _____  Hector Suco    Date: _____

# Remarrying After Divorce

This worksheet is strictly for anyone who is divorced and wants to remarry. If you lost a partner and are planning to remarry, please use my Finding Partnership After Loss Worksheet. Lastly, if you have lost a partner <u>and</u> have been divorced (2 or more separate marriages), and are planning to get married a third, fourth… time, use this worksheet to reflect on your divorces only.

1. Age: _____

2. What is your relationship status?
    - ☐ Dating someone consistently
    - ☐ In a relationship
    - ☐ Engaged

2A. How long have you and your new partner been together? _____

3. This will be your _____ marriage.
                         (number)

3A. This will be your partner's _____ marriage.
                                    (number)

4. List the reasons you think your past marriages did not work out.

_____

_____

_____

5. How will things be different this time? How will **you** be different this time?

_____

_____

_____

6. How does your partner feel about your past marriage(s)?

_____

_____

7. Are you/your partner bringing any children into this marriage?
☐ Yes (Go to 7A)
☐ No (Go to 8)

7A. How many? _____

7B. How do your children feel about this marriage?

_____

_____

_____

8. How is this marriage going to be different than your previous marriage(s)?

_____

_____

_____

9. What are some of your goals as a future married couple as compared to your last marriage?

_____

_____

Name: _____  Hector Suco  Date: _____

# Remarrying After Divorce

This worksheet is strictly for anyone who is divorced and wants to remarry. If you lost a partner and are planning to remarry, please use my Finding Partnership After Loss Worksheet. Lastly, if you have lost a partner <u>and</u> have been divorced (2 or more separate marriages), and are planning to get married a third, fourth… time, use this worksheet to reflect on your divorces only.

1. Age: _____

2. What is your relationship status?
    - ☐ Dating someone consistently
    - ☐ In a relationship
    - ☐ Engaged

2A. How long have you and your new partner been together? _____

3. This will be your _____ marriage.
                        (number)

3A. This will be your partner's _____ marriage.
                                      (number)

4. List the reasons you think your past marriages did not work out.

_____

_____

_____

5. How will things be different this time? How will **you** be different this time?

_____

_____

_____

6. How does your partner feel about your past marriage(s)?

_____

_____

7. Are you/your partner bringing any children into this marriage?
☐ Yes (Go to 7A)
☐ No (Go to 8)

7A. How many? _____

7B. How do your children feel about this marriage?

_____
_____
_____

8. How is this marriage going to be different than your previous marriage(s)?

_____
_____
_____

9. What are some of your goals as a future married couple as compared to your last marriage?

_____
_____

# Remarrying After Divorce Worksheet Guide

2A. The length of time that you have been in this relationship is a factor. Some will want to get right to it and tie the knot, but the last thing you want to do is rush into a marriage. Be happy at this stage in your life and progress at your own pace.

3. Do you and/or your partner have a problem with the number of past marriages each of you have had?

4. "Yes, the past can hurt. But the way I see it, you can either run from it or learn from it."
-Rafiki, from the film *The Lion King*

You should try to learn from your past mistakes if you want this one to work. What went wrong? Why?

5. Do not only blame your past partners. Look inside yourself and explain what went wrong with you and why. Once you do that, you learn from your mistakes and try to never let it happen again.

6. Leave your past baggage at the door as you start your new relationship. Make sure your partner is okay with the fact that you have been married before.

7. Bringing a new partner around your children can be tricky. If your children have a good relationship with your new partner, then the announcement of your upcoming marriage should be a happy occasion. Write down how you think your children feel about this new marriage. If you do not know, ask them, their opinions can be insightful.

8. There are many factors that contribute to a happy marriage. What can you improve upon from your last marriage? What can you change? What do you think you should continue doing?
Examples include:

| Constant Communication | keeping the finances transparent | making time for dates | Seeing a marriage counselor |
|---|---|---|---|
| Saying "I love you" consistently with meaning | Buying thoughtful gifts | Exploring your sexuality and your partner's | Sit-down dinners every night with the family |

9. Examples include:

| Better/More Sex | Better/More Communication | Getting out of debt | Better social life together | Having children |
|---|---|---|---|---|
| Take more vacations | Go on more Dates | Save more money | Say "I love you" more often | More quality family time |
| Work less | Spend more alone time together | Add more romance. | Share chores | More intimacy |

I hope this has helped you.
Good luck on your journey.

Name: _____  Hector Suco  Date: _____

# Loss Of Partner

Please accept my deepest condolences.

1. Where are you in the 5 Stages of Grief?

☐ Denial    ☐ Anger    ☐ Bargaining    ☐ Depression    ☐ Acceptance

2. Do you believe in God? If not, go to #5        ☐ Yes        ☐ No

3. Do you believe in an afterlife, like Heaven?    ☐ Yes        ☐ No

4. Do you believe your loved one is "up" there, looking down at you?

    ☐ Yes        ☐ No

5. While your loved one was alive, do you feel that you made the most of your time together?    ☐ Yes    ☐ No

6. Do you believe things will get better?    ☐ Yes        ☐ No

\* If you chose "no" for #5 and/or #6, please write why you feel this way.

_____

_____

7. What are some things you are feeling? What physical or emotional symptoms are you experiencing?

_____

_____

_____

_____

8. If your loved one were present right now, what would you say to them?

_____

_____

_____

_____

9. If your loved one were present in this room right now, what do you think they would say to you?

_____

_____

_____

_____

Name: _____    Hector Suco    Date: _____

# Loss Of Partner

Please accept my deepest condolences.

1. Where are you in the 5 Stages of Grief?

☐ Denial   ☐ Anger   ☐ Bargaining   ☐ Depression   ☐ Acceptance

2. Do you believe in God? If not, go to #5     ☐ Yes     ☐ No

3. Do you believe in an afterlife, like Heaven?   ☐ Yes   ☐ No

4. Do you believe your loved one is "up" there, looking down at you?

☐ Yes     ☐ No

5. While your loved one was alive, do you feel that you made the most of your time together?     ☐ Yes     ☐ No

6. Do you believe things will get better?     ☐ Yes     ☐ No

\* If you chose "no" for #5 and/or #6, please write why you feel this way.

_____

_____

7. What are some things you are feeling? What physical or emotional symptoms are you experiencing?

_____

_____

_____

8. If your loved one were present right now, what would you say to them?

_____

_____

_____

_____

9. If your loved one were present in this room right now, what do you think they would say to you?

_____

_____

_____

_____

# Loss of Partner Worksheet Guide

1. Recognizing where you are in the 5 stages of loss can benefit you through this tough time. Note that not everyone goes through the five stages in order; some may skip a stage or stages.

2. When all seems lost, some ask why. Has your relationship with God changed? Do you believe in Him more or less? The same?

3. Many religions believe in an afterlife. Heaven is described as a place that our loved ones go when they pass away. They do not cease to exist; they are taken to a better place where they keep an eye on us.

4. Do you believe that they are in your presence? Do you believe you are in their presence? Do they hear you? Feel you? Sense you?

5. This is an important factor as you try to cope with loss. If the answer is no, then be clear as to why you feel this way in the space below. This is a form of guilt that you may have.

6. If you picked no, I would advise you to seek medical attention.

7. Examples include:

| Shock | Numb |
|---|---|
| Fear | Angry |
| Guilty that I'm still alive | Hard to make decisions |
| Low concentration | Trouble sleeping |
| Loss of appetite | Sadness |

8. Use the space provided to express any feelings of regret, pain, or your sense of yearning for your loved one.

- "I miss you"
- "I wish you were here."
- "I love you"
- "It is not the same without you."
- "I'll see you soon"
- "Thank you for looking after me."
- "Say hi to [other deceased] for me

9. Examples include:

- "Do not cry over me, I am okay. I am in a better place."
- "I am not in pain."
- "I will always look after you."
- "I am home now, go on. Live your best life."
- "Let go; Move on without me."
- "Look after our children."
- "Look after [living relative(s)] for me."
- "Promise me… "
- "Remember when…"


I hope this has helped you.
Good luck on your journey.

Name: _____    Hector Suco    Date: _____

# Finding Partnership After Loss

1. What was your relationship status with your partner when they passed away?

☐ Couple   ☐ Engaged   ☐ Married

2. Did you and your partner ever discuss finding love if one of you were to pass away? If so, what was your partner's opinion on the matter? What is your opinion?

_____

_____

3. What are your conditions for letting another person enter your life and potentially your heart?

_____

_____

_____

_____

4. Are you currently dating someone?

☐ Yes (Go to #5, Skip #9)   ☐ No (Go to #9)

5. Is this person a constant in your life?

☐ Yes (Go to #6)   ☐ No (Go to #10)

6. Have you discussed your loss with them?

☐ Yes
☐ No: When do you plan to? _____

7. Does this person accept the "conditions" you wrote down for #3 in regards to remembering your past partner?

☐ Yes (Go to #8, Skip #9)   ☐ No (Answer #7A & 8, Skip #9)

7A. Have they told you why they have not accepted these conditions?

_____

_____

8. Are you willing to take the next step in your new relationship?

☐ Yes: What is the next step for your relationship? _____

☐ No: Why not?

_____

_____

9. What is stopping you from dating?

_____

_____

_____

10. Do you believe your partner is in a "better place"?

☐ Yes (Go to #11)  ☐ No (Go to #12)

11. Do you believe they are in tune with what's going on in your life, wherever they are?

☐ Yes  ☐ No

12. What do you think your partner would want for you now that they are not around?

_____

_____

_____

Name: _____     Hector Suco     Date: _____

# Finding Partnership After Loss

1. What was your relationship status with your partner when they passed away?

☐  Couple          ☐  Engaged          ☐  Married

2. Did you and your partner ever discuss finding love if one of you were to pass away? If so, what was your partner's opinion on the matter? What is your opinion?

_____

_____

3. What are your conditions for letting another person enter your life and potentially your heart?

_____

_____

_____

_____

4. Are you currently dating someone?

☐  Yes (Go to #5, Skip #9)          ☐  No (Go to #9)

5. Is this person a constant in your life?

☐  Yes (Go to #6)          ☐  No (Go to #10)

6. Have you discussed your loss with them?
☐  Yes
☐  No: When do you plan to? _____

7. Does this person accept the "conditions" you wrote down for #3 in regards to remembering your past partner?

☐  Yes (Go to #8, Skip #9)          ☐  No (Answer #7A & 8, Skip #9)

7A. Have they told you why they have not accepted these conditions?

_____

_____

8. Are you willing to take the next step in your new relationship?

☐   Yes: What is the next step for your relationship? _____

☐   No: Why not?

_____

_____

9. What is stopping you from dating?

_____

_____

_____

10. Do you believe your partner is in a "better place"?

☐   Yes (Go to #11)          ☐   No (Go to #12)

11. Do you believe they are in tune with what's going on in your life, wherever they are?

☐   Yes                       ☐   No

12. What do you think your partner would want for you now that they are not around?

_____

_____

_____

_____

# Finding Partnership After Loss Worksheet Guide

2. Some people will say that they want their partner to eventually find love with someone else if they were to pass away, even if they would hope there was a certain period of time between their passing and the new love. Some people would want their partners to move on right away. This all differs from person to person and couple to couple.

3. Some examples of spoken or unspoken agreements include:

| I will never "move on." I will always remember my partner. | My children will always come first. | My children will not call you Mom/Dad. |
|---|---|---|
| I will always have a relationship with my late partner's family. | Has to accept the situation. | My children may call you Mom/Dad. |
| I will not change my last name. | I may change my last name. ||
| Know that if my spouse were alive, I would not be with you. |||

*Source:* www.alongthebrokenroad.com

4. You should only begin to date when you are ready. Do not feel bad if you are not seeing anyone yet or do not want to.

5. Make sure that if you are dating someone consistently, that they accept your "conditions" as stated in #3.

6. Discussing your late partner is important, especially if your conditions from #3 say so. Your late spouse still being a part of your life in some way may not be okay with your new loved one. How often you talk about your late partner with your new partner is up to the both of you to decide. Respect their wishes if they are not comfortable having these types of conversations yet or at all.

7. If your new love interest does not meet all the conditions, they may not be the one for you. That is not their fault and it is not your fault, either. If you believe that this person may start to accept your loss and how you cope with it over time, you may want to slow things down to give them more time to adjust to the idea.

8. If your new love interest is accepting of how you feel about your loss, then you may want to take the relationship to the next level if you are ready. If you are not ready to take this relationship to the next level, that is okay. Take all the time you need.

9. Examples include:

| I am waiting until I am ready. | I am afraid to move on. |
|---|---|
| I am afraid of opening up my heart again | I do not think my previous partner wants me to start seeing other people. |
| No one will ever replace my previous partner. | I have too many other things going on. |

10. & 11. Many religions believe in an afterlife. Heaven is described as a place that our loved ones go when they pass away. Their bodies may die, but their souls live on. They watch over us.

12. Write down what you think they would want from you as you live the rest of your life. Writing this down may help put things into perspective.

Sometimes, people who know they are dying decide to leave something behind in the form of words, video, etc. If your partner has done this, keep it close to your heart as you slowly figure out how to live life without them.

I hope this has helped you.
Good luck on your journey.

# Afterword

My ultimate goal is for you to be happy. Whether that's you being single or in a relationship. I believe happiness is the meaning to our lives. One cannot live fully if they are not happy and content. I hope that this book was able to get you to that point.

Sincerely,
Hector Suco

# Acknowledgements

This book would not have been possible without the love and support of my beautiful wife, Lucia Suco. She has stood by me throughout the whole process. I thank her for her wisdom, advice and love.

# About The Author

Hector Suco was born and raised in Miami, FL. He attended Florida International University and graduated with a degree in Education in 2009. He also attended Miami Dade College and graduated with a degree in Film in 2014. He is currently a middle school teacher. He is married to his wife, Lucia Suco. They have two children.

Hector Suco is the author of 4 books and 2 eBooks. He also has a motivational spoken word album titled "Life Lessons." You may search "Hector Suco" on Amazon.com for all of his products. He also has an array of online courses on achieving your goals, stress mastery, finding your happiness, helping others with their relationships, and much more. You may search "Hector Suco" on Udemy.com for all of his online courses.

Go to HectorSucoSpeaker.com for more information.

www.ingramcontent.com/pod-product-compliance
Lightning Source LLC
Chambersburg PA
CBHW080454110426
42742CB00017B/2890